PERSON AND SOCIETY

DUQUESNE STUDIES

Theological Series

5

PERSON AND SOCIETY
A Christian View

by

JOHN H. WALGRAVE, O.P., S.T.D.

DUQUESNE UNIVERSITY PRESS

Pittsburgh, Pa.

EDITIONS E. NAUWELAERTS, LOUVAIN

DUQUESNE STUDIES

THEOLOGICAL SERIES

Henry J. Koren, C.S.Sp., S.T.D., Leonard A. Bushinski, C.S.Sp., M.A., S.T.L., Leonard J. Swidler, Ph.D., S.T.L., editors.

Volume One—*Albert Dondeyne,* FAITH AND THE WORLD. XI and 324 pages. Price: $5.00 cloth.

Volume Two—*Peter Schoonenberg, S.J.,* GOD'S WORLD IN THE MAKING. IX and 207 pages. Price: $3.95 cloth.

Volume Three—*Leonard J. Swidler, editor,* SCRIPTURE AND ECUMENISM. VII and 197 pages. Price: $4.95 cloth.

Volume Four—*William H. van de Pol, S.T.D.,* ANGLICANISM IN ECUMENICAL PERSPECTIVE. X and 293 pages. Price: $6.75 cloth.

Volume Five—*John H. Walgrave, O.P., S.T.D.,* PERSON AND SOCIETY. 182 pages. Price: $4.25 cloth.

In preparation:

Fundamentals and Programs of a New Catechesis
Henry Fries, *Bultmann-Barth and Catholic Theology*

Nihil Obstat

Rev. William J. Winter, S.T.D.
Censor Librorum

Imprimatur

†Most Rev. Vincent M. Leonard, D.D.
Vicar General—Chancellor

Library of Congress Catalog Card Number 65—22936

TABLE OF CONTENTS

Table of Contents

Table of Contents

CHAPTER SEVEN—Socio-Ethical Principles

PREFACE

Starting from man's existential need to understand the meaning of his life, the author sees man as placed midway between the ideals of life presented by Revelation and reason, on the one hand, and the historical limitations of his situated existence, on the other. Thus, in his attempts to realize his ideals, it becomes man's dynamic task to humanize himself and his world through the full flowering of his personality. As a social being, however, man can humanize himself and his world only by loving and respecting his fellow-men as persons and by creating, together with them, an ever-growing human community of love. This community must be governed by solidarity, social freedom and authentic respect of all for all.

The original edition of this book was published in Dutch as the introduction to a four volume set entitled *Welfare, Well-being and Happiness.* It was translated by Walter van de Putte, C.S.Sp., carefully revised by the undersigned, and submitted to the author for his approval. Indexes have been added to this edition.

Duquesne University   HENRY J. KOREN, C.S.Sp

CHAPTER ONE

UNITY AND DUALITY OF THE CHRISTIAN VIEW OF LIFE

1. THE SEARCH FOR THE NORM

The Christian view regarding our social relations is one aspect of the total Christian view about man. An organic unity joins the diverse aspects of that view into a single coherent whole. For this reason the social view of Christianity can be approached only from the standpoint of that total view if we wish to understand it better.

A "Christian view of man" means a coherent ensemble of ideas about man, about his nature, his life, his lot and destiny, his relation to nature, to his fellow-man and to God. Hence that view is itself a part of a universal all-embracing Christian view of the world. The latter has grown as a tradition bearing a historical character. We are well aware that today's "Christian view of man" is not to be equated with a collection of unchangeable supra-historical truths. We are ready to distinguish between a core, a central zone of absolute truth, and a marginal zone of Christian opinion that is proper to the historical period in which we are living in the same way as former Christian opinions were proper to their period of history. Nor are we reluctant to make a further distinction between the content of that core and the ways of formulating it. Certain formulas, even of absolutely fundamental truths, are susceptible of improvement or of restatement in new expressions. We readily admit that our minds lack a complete grasp of the mystery which is the content of our faith; the human mind never succeeds in gaining complete possession of what is given to it. There is always room for further clarification, for making things more explicit, for introducing nuances, for further developments.

Accordingly, what we designate by a "Christian view of man" is subject to criticism. Hence there arises the question

11

regarding a norm of judgment. Where shall we find a solid basis on which to discern what belongs or does not belong to the Christian vision, what must be preserved as the un-changeable core and what pertains to the relative domain of opinion and manner of expression?

To a Christian, the answer to that question does not, at first sight, seem particularly difficult. He sees that norm in Revelation, which dawned slowly in the history of Israel and finally broke through like a sun in the manifestation of Christ. The Christian view of man is the one that was unveiled to us in Christ and is now further preserved and unfolded by the Church. We find that view objectively in Sacred Scripture and in the living tradition of faith, under the guidance of the Church's teaching authority.

2. THINKING EXISTENCE IN SEARCH OF ITSELF

The question, however, is not as simple as that. For Revelation is not the sole constituent of our Christian view of man and society. Revelation presupposes another factor, man and his conscious life. Only on the basis of his con-scious life is man capable of discovering Revelation and giving meaning to it. Now, conscious life is a life that is aware of itself. Consciousness is precisely a being-with-one-self, by which man, prior to reflection, already possesses an immediate experience of the existence he has in the world. This being-conscious, this life that is present to itself, is for us the only access to any understanding of things.

In the lived encounter with things and men there arise in us images and ideas by which we interpret to ourselves our life and also the reality in which we live. In this way the world that is first merely "lived" becomes a "thought" world, a represented world; it becomes put in order and expressed by means of the word. This world is our own world. We know no other. Our immediate experience of the world is taken up into our interpretation of the world; we reach the former only in and through the latter. The latter is not a world that stands apart, a world of independently existing ideas that takes the place of the immediately experienced world. This "thought" world is an ordering that gives meaning to what we have experienced. It is "intentional"; it is nothing but our complete human consciousness of the world of immediate experience.

It should be clear that the term "experience" is used in a special sense. In philosophical writings, the term has various meanings which should be carefully distinguished. Without going into the matter, let us simply state our meaning in the present context.

"Experience" in the strict sense in which it is used here is one aspect of human consciousness, opposed to another that we call "thought." Experience may be taken also in a broader sense. It then comprises both experience in the strict sense and thought, in the unity of conscious existence, insofar as that existence is immediately present to the existent.

It is, then, one of the philosophical assumptions of this essay that the whole of our conscious existence (consciousness of a world and our presence in that world) is constituted by two activities which compenetrate each other intimately. The first we call "experience" in the strict or narrow sense. It is an immediate cognitive contact with the reality of our existence and with the realities that enter into our existence. It does not coincide with sensation, as in the Kantian point of view. Sensation is but one aspect of it, one moment, indicating the embodied side of a mode of consciousness that, although dependent on an organism, is not reducible to organic activity.

Experience in that sense, although more recondite, is the primary, the most original and fundamental aspect of our conscious being. It is the background and condition for the exercise of "thought." By "thought" we mean the busy, discursive aspect of consciousness in its spontaneous as well as in its deliberate exercise. It is the creative source of all distinct ideas and relations by means of which experience is objectified, explicitated and ordered into a world of mental perception. In it lies the origin of language and of

13

the intricate and plastic relational system of meanings attached to language.

"Thought" is the restless attempt of conscious existence to grasp and appropriate the fullness of that which presents itself in experience. Its aim is a life that possesses itself, able to go its own ways according to definite conceptions and precise, self-made projects.

The typical restlessness of thought is a clear indication that experience is ever present to the thinking mind as an inviting and transcendent awareness. In real living thought we are immediately aware of the presence of experience which stimulates and permeates all the spontaneous developments as well as the conative and deliberate endeavors of our thinking activity. Experience is the inexhaustible "stuff" out of which thought makes its tools and its products, ever reshaping, adjusting and refining them.

It is clear, then, that experience and thought are intimately one. They are two aspects of the whole of conscious life always permeating each other. In the first aspect, that of experience, our conscious life is rather given to us; in the second, that of thought, it is made by us. The first is originating, the second is originated. Experience and thought encompass the whole of our conscious life.

Experience, then, is not a first mode of knowing that gathers data for subsequent thinking and reasoning, as was held by Lockian empiricism. Its object is the totality of that which is present to conscious existence and is to be explored and conquered by thought. Thought, even when it makes mistakes, always aims at experience as the source and rule of truth, and without experience it would be immobilized. Experience, on the other hand, calls for thought in order to become explicit, and without thought it would have no distinct content for the conscious subject.

The totality of that which presents itself in experience and which becomes the object of explicitating and interpreting thought we call "world." Consequently we distinguish between a world of immediate experience and a world of thought. But, as experience and thought are one, so also are the worlds corresponding to either of them.

In our ordinary existence we are not aware of two worlds, of one immediately experienced and another created by thought. The world we "think" is for us the truth and the reality of the world we experience. It is only in philosophical reflection that we can make clear the distinction between life as we immediately experience it, and life as we view it in our thoughts. My world forms a unity of immediate awareness and explanatory thought. My consciousness of the world is always a view of the world. My consciousness of life is always a view of life. To live in the world is at once to live within a definite view of existence.

Hence every man lives within a total view of existence. Although within this view men can distinguish diverse aspects and factors, at the center there is always the view of his own being-man, of his relation to the total reality in which he lives and to the various kinds of reality that constitute the whole of reality. Man, in a certain sense, cannot help being at the center of his thought. For his life is the standpoint from which he becomes conscious of everything else. He is unable to free himself from that point of view, for he himself is that standpoint.

His lived and self-thinking existence in the world is for him the only gate through which he can reach anything. The experience of his own life is his total experience because every experience is experience only to the extent that it occurs within conscious existence. The clarification of his view of the world by means of thought takes place in function of a clarification that his own existence demands of him. "The proper study of mankind is man."

The human world is not a private world although it is a world shaped by thought. It is, first of all, a common, a social world. We are not born simply as biological beings in a natural world. As men we enter into existence in a cultural world; we awake to conscious existence in a world that has already been clarified and ordered in a definite way by others. Through the language we learn, we enter into the world of

15

our culture, our time, our generation. Unconsciously we partake of that world as it sinks into us and permeates us through education and the ordinary contacts of daily life. When we reach the age of true personal existence, a definite world, shaped mainly by tradition, has already taken possession of our minds, controlling them by its apparent self-evidence and unquestionableness. Our view of the world, of man, is inevitably social. For this reason we can speak of a Chinese view of man, a Buddhist or a Christian view.

In this world of tradition we can remain until our death as in an unquestionable reality without any serious reflection, without asking questions or troubling ourselves with problems. But it is also possible by personal thought to make our own what has been transmitted by tradition, and thus rise to a critical consent to that world in which we begin to exist. Or we can change that world for ourselves, so that our personal world becomes a somewhat modified version of the common social world. We can also repudiate it, and try to establish another world in contrast with the traditional understanding of the world. Finally, we can decide to go over to the world of another tradition, although to what extent we will be successful in this attempt is another question.

We live in a world of which we not only take possession by our thinking, but in which we must also always continue to search and to transform it to the best of our ability. Our existence always continues to ask and seek meaning. We do not possess our existence as a heritage that has been clarified once and for all; we ourselves are possessed by it as a mystery that constantly calls for further clarification. Although the thought world is patterned on our lived world and is intended to reveal this world truthfully, we realize that our thought world does not reveal the total reality. There are more things in heaven and on earth than our thinking can clarify. Our world is a never finished project for our thought. Even the certainty of the world of our faith, says St. Thomas in agreement with St. Augustine, does not exclude the *cogitatio,* the questioning and searching thought.

3. Existential Need

The most profound driving power of our thinking and seeking existence, is existential need. We simply have to think about the world, for otherwise it is not possible for us to live in it. In the various situations of our life we cannot simply commit ourselves to the guidance of our unconscious nature, for, lacking the inborn wisdom of instinct, it is ignorant. Having no unconscious wisdom of nature, we are obliged to proceed by means of a conscious wisdom. This wisdom is not innate in us; hence we must try to find it and develop it. Thinking is for man the indispensable substitute for instinct, the means that enables man to live. Our thought is a life that is "self-thinking" because we are uncertain about ourselves. Hence human existence as originally given to us is bewilderment, trouble and care.

Man, then, is constantly faced with all sorts of problems that are difficult to solve. His existence is a problem. A variety of questions constantly arise regarding his existence. There is first the question of self-preservation in the material world. This world offers many possibilities for his corporal life, and alternately presents all kinds of dangers. By thinking he must learn to know the possibilities and to discern the dangers; he must also learn how to exploit those possibilities ever better and how to overcome the dangers in a more efficient way. This is the origin of exact knowledge of the world around us (*Umwelt*) and of technology.

Secondly, on the level of self-conscious being, life as a whole, the contingent fact of existence, ceases to be something to be taken for granted. Why are we living? For what purpose are we living? What makes life worth living? To ask questions such as these belongs to the very nature of man, to his being-man. Added to concern about his sustenance, then, is the spiritual unrest that characterizes man so profoundly. He is a "metaphysical animal." He must have an answer to the question concerning the meaning of reality and of his life; he must find a fundamental value that can justify his contingent and unasked-for existence in the world.

Life is, in itself, a value but to man it becomes a value only when he knows it as such and consents to it.

Thirdly, for a conscious being not only existence itself but also any situation, as an invitation to action, loses its unquestionableness. Self-conscious existence threatens man with the danger of loneliness, of separation from the whole of being and from other self-conscious beings. He will not be able to remain in harmony with the whole and with society if he cannot justify to himself why it is better to act or not to act in various circumstances, or to act in this way or another. Hence, ethical thinking is also a part of man's being.

We see, then, that man's view of reality has various aspects. There is a physical view of the world that is directed to useful ends; a metaphysical idea of the world that gives meaning to conscious existence; and an ethical conception of life that guides his behavior in the world in a meaningful way. This manifold view of reality is nothing but a view concerning man himself in his manifold relationship with reality.

4. Historical Dialectics and Freedom That Creates Culture

Human life is characterized by historicity. The radical difference between instinctive existence and self-conscious existence is that the former merely undergoes the world in which it is living, whereas the latter intervenes in the world and changes it in a creative way. Instinctive life is wholly encompassed by nature—organisms governed by laws in a world of law and regularity. The interaction of instinct and environment (*Umwelt*) is likewise prescribed by strict laws. Thus the course of instinctive existence is completely woven into the course of universal nature.

By contrast, self-conscious life is a free life. According to the universal and unsophisticated evidence of human consciousness, we do not perceive mere sense phenomena but real independent things which constitute a real world, existing in its own right. To acknowledge this is the only true and radical "empiricism." Moreover, it is the only key to a coherent comprehension of the various aspects of the "human phenomenon," i.e., of all that is proper to man as such. For by his consciousness of a world "out there," man takes a stand before the world as a real subject before an object. Thus he acquires his subjective irreducibility, his unique standpoint, which he calls his "I."

From that self-conscious standpoint he is aware of the world as an objective reality. At the same time man does not merely discover the world as something factual that must be taken into account, but he learns to know it also as a wealth of possibilities to be actualized by his activity. Not only is the world that forms the object of thought an interpretation of what the lived world is and signifies, but it is also a project of practical meanings which we can and desire to fulfill. Man knows his situation not only as something that is given and to which he must adapt himself, but also as something adaptable to his needs and desires.

This power to create culture, which enables man to change his situation in the world, is the source of historicity, in which the proper character of his being-man manifests itself. For by constantly changing his situation, man also creates ever new problems which, in their turn, require new considerations and reflections thus inviting him to a new exercise of his creative power.

In this way the historical course of human existence is truly dialectical. There is a constant interaction between freedom's operative intervention and the resulting existential situation, a reciprocal influence that cannot be brought to a standstill, and by which mankind is driven ever further toward an unknown goal. Man modifies his world according to his ideas. That changed world calls up new problems in his existence, and these problems force him to counter them with new ideas. This process continues endlessly.

The historical dialectics frequently lead to dramatic moments. Throwing man into despair, they often oblige him to reexamine thoroughly his interpretation of existence. The crisis affects not only his exact knowledge of nature but also

19

his idea of the world and of life. Copernicus' discovery, for example, brought about a complete revolution in our ideas of cosmic nature, and that revolution, in turn, caused a crisis in the traditional world view. What is man's place, as a dweller upon earth, in that limitless universe in which the earth has lost its central position? Where are Heaven and Hell? What is the meaning of the Resurrection and Ascension of Christ? Is it still possible for us to speak of an "above" and a "hereafter"? Is there still room for an immortal soul? Pascal had already a clear perception of those problems. Giordano Bruno and Spinoza were prompted by them to propose new world views. And is it not true that the questions related to those problems continue to plague the mind of man even in our own day? The passionate debate, raised all over the world by Dr. John Robinson's *Honest to God,* should warn us how serious these problems remain.

The experiments that have led to the development of nuclear physics also brought about a revolution in our concepts of matter and the nature of the cosmos. But the consequences of those discoveries raise new questions. For instance, the existence of nuclear weapons makes war an entirely new problem. Even the very concept of war can no longer remain unchanged in our atomic age. Planetary unification and world peace bring up moral problems that are dictated by the progress of science and technology.

The reverse is equally true: our view of the world and of life constantly influences the evolution of physical science and technology. Reality as we think it does not coincide with reality as it is present in our original experience, but is always an incomplete interpretation of it. For this reason, in our attempts to live in the world according to our ideas, we always meet new problems which we are unable to solve with the principles we have in store. Every attempt to synthesize our experience in an orderly system of ideas, on the basis of definite principles and according to particular methods, reveals its deficiencies after a while. We are then caught in insoluble problems and see how the mystery of reality ironically breaks through and disrupts our categories.

Such crises inspire movements of scepticism and disenchanted pleas to return to the so-called unadulterated facts of experience. For example, during late scholasticism, unsuccessful speculations about nature led to the scepticism of the nominalists and was followed by an attempt to study the immediately observable connection of natural phenomena without worrying about philosophical ideas. On the other hand, the extreme volatile character of man's knowledge of God in nominalistic theology turned interest away from heavenly and divine things and toward man and his problems of life on earth. Thus there occurred a twofold historical revolution: the method went from speculation to observation, and man's interest switched from heaven to earthly things. From the union of these two was born the modern spirit with its earthly humanism and its esteem for the empirical and the technical.

Accordingly, the fact that Western man did turn so strongly toward technological mastery over nature was fundamentally determined by deeper changes in his view of the world. Even the further development of the physical sciences is influenced, as is now rather generally admitted, by philosophical ideas.[1]

In this way the restless pendulum of our total thought swings back and forth between various realms of knowledge in which we try to explain the many aspects of existence. Man's view and vision are constantly changing. History reveals man to himself in the many dimensions of his life. And the mainspring of history is man's restless questioning regarding his own being, his destiny and the meaning of his life.

The answer is not given by the mind alone but by the whole adventure of our historical existence. Just as man moves as a whole in all genuine thinking, so is the whole

---

[1]Cf. Andrew G. van Melsen, *From Atomos to Atom*, Pittsburgh, 1952; *Science and Technology*, Pittsburgh, 1961. Tr.

of culture involved in its spiritual movement. Every new situation opens another window through which man gets a new view of himself. At every turn of life there awaits the possibility of a fresh insight and truth if he is willing to recognize and accept the light of that moment.

5. INDEPENDENT HISTORICAL EXISTENCE AND DIVINE REVELATION

Man's existence is a self-thinking existence; that is why no Christian view of man can be a pure datum of Revelation. A Christian view is possible only as a living synthesis born from the encounter between the man who tries to fathom his existence and God who expresses His judgment about man and reveals to him the meaning that He Himself gives to human life.

Thus Revelation presupposes an existence that, on the ground of a certain self-understanding, continues to seek and question itself. A closed self-complacency is not open to a divine Revelation. Christ Himself made a distinction between men who have ears to hear and eyes to see, and others, who are deaf to God's word and blind to His manifestation. God's Revelation can be heard in history only when there is a living questioning on the part of man. That is why Revelation itself manifests an historical character.

If God's Revelation is a *kairos,* a critical moment for man, definite moments in history are also a *kairos;* they are an opportune time for Revelation. We know, of course, that God's Providence directs the whole movement, that the moments He chooses are themselves called up by Him in history. But we who behold the encounter of God and man from a standpoint within history, must make a distinction between the immanent movement of history and the intervention of the transcendent God in its course.

Revelation is historical. Its course from Adam to Christ was marked by contingency. It was prepared in the early history of Israel and gradually became clearer in the adventures of the chosen people. The Old Testament Revelation was not arbitrarily inserted in the development of Israel. God's words did not fall upon the spirits of His people like meteorites. There was an intimate connection between the immanent movement of Jewish history and the interventions of the transcendent God. We notice a dramatic coherence between word and response: the infidelity of the people and the fidelity of God, the historical need and God's merciful intervention, the prayers of the faithful and the promises of salvation. God seized in history the *kairos,* the opportune time that was offered Him, and there He placed His word as a *kairos,* an opportune message for man. For instance, the exodus from Egypt was God's moment for the Covenant; the Babylonian Captivity was for Him the proper time for purifying and raising Israel's ideas by means of His prophets, and for inspiring a longing attention to the coming of the Anointed One.

God's word wrapped itself in the garments of historical situation. God spoke the language of the particular time. He adjusted Himself to the spirit of Israel. If His word at first sounds primitive and then gradually grows more spiritual, it is because God adapted Himself to the degree of development of His chosen people. He spoke to them through them and used the patterns and categories of their own way of thinking.

Christ Himself appeared, as the final Revelation of God, in the "fullness of the times," that is, in a historical *kairos,* at the right moment that God had carefully prepared beforehand. He came when the Roman Empire had reached its maximum development and thus prefigured the Church in her catholicity, that is, a unity within a diversity of peoples, languages and cultures. Only in that situation was it possible for the one word of God to be heard and understood on Pentecost by each of the many peoples in their own tongue.

Revelation does not appear in history merely as a reply from the transcendent realm to questions that live and ripen to maturity in the immanent movement of history. This movement itself becomes, under the invitation of God's word, a constant reply to man: he either closes or opens himself for God's message; he listens or stops his ears; He understands or persists in his misunderstanding; He believes or remains in a sceptical attitude, clinging to his narrow, purely human insight; he obeys or rebels; he goes Godward or turns away from Him.

Accordingly, the history of salvation is similarly dialectical: to the existence of man who searches for meaning and is exposed to the danger of losing himself in insoluble riddles, there comes an answer from God's mystery of Revelation. This answer forces man to take a stand and reflect anew on his existence. But this reflection in the light of God's word also leads to ever new questions that seek ever new replies on the part of God.

6. Dialectical Development of Understanding Through Faith

We do not mean that new direct revelations were made to the Church after Christ and the Apostles. In Christ shines the light that not only comes from God Himself. God, in the form of man, "one tried as we are" (Hebr. 4:15), lived his earthly life as an example of perfect religious obedience. In that one form is definitively revealed the fundamental truth of God and the fundamental truth about man. Through the understanding of faith bestowed upon the Apostles by the Holy Spirit, mankind has appropriated the apparition of God in Christ according to its true meaning. In this respect nothing more is to be added to God's Revelation.

However, that truth of Revelation, concentrated in a living form in Christ and faithfully mirrored in the charismatic belief of the Apostles and inspired writers, will be unfolded and developed in the believing thought of the Church until the final coming of Christ. That unfolding is historical. It is guided and guaranteed by the Holy Spirit, whose invisible guidance encompasses the whole history of salvation.

24

Furthermore, this development did not stop with the Ascension of Christ, but by the sending of the Holy Spirit merely entered into a new phase. The Church's history remains a history of salvation until the end of time and that history of salvation is at the same time a historical unveiling of the mystery of Christ in the thinking of the Church.

Nor is this thinking the work of the mind alone, but the fruit of the whole life of the Church. The Church too moves as a whole in her dogmatic and theological explanation of the faith. Her concrete movement is not accomplished solely by faith, by obedience, by the active fidelity and the zealous efforts of responsible Christians. It manifests also the shadows and hesitations of our weak faith, our self-will and stubbornness, our selfish conservatism and passionate narrow-mindedness, our cowardly infidelity, sloth and self-complacency. How often did not the Christians let slip by unused the *kairos* of God's word at critical moments of history! The light shone in the darkness but the darkness grasped it not; did not receive it loyally and accept it with enthusiasm.

Just as the history of civilization shows a dialectical movement in which man's freedom and the particular features of his situation dramatically affect one another, so does the history of salvation manifest a movement in which our vacillating efforts and the power of God's word merge through constant interaction into a single dramatic event. And, as reflective existence in the world of natural experience constantly clarifies the mystery of existence through conflict with ever new situations, so too does reflective existence in the world of faith, through a confrontation with the varying circumstances of the Church's history, gradually lead to a clarification of the mystery of Christ. The two are now one, for the history of salvation from now on encompasses the whole of history, both in its relative failures and its successes.

7. DUALITY AND UNITY OF CHRISTIAN THOUGHT

In that all-encompassing movement and commitment, Christian thought manifests two aspects: it is a reflection upon the faith and a reflection upon the earthly problems of life in the light of the faith. On the one hand, there is the work of theological reflection trying to unfold and explain Revelation in a meaningful system. On the other, there is Christian reflection in all fields of human activity and the attempt to understand the concrete historical situations of our variable earthly existence in a spirit of faith, in order that Christian culture give a creative answer to contemporary problems. These two undertakings are intimately connected and influence each other. It is evident, for instance, that the modern idea of evolution has purified and clarified our theological concept of the first chapters of Genesis. It has also helped us understand that dogmatic tradition is characterized by development. Again, we see clearly that man's situation in modern society has acted as a stimulus in bringing to the foreground and giving a more firm structure and development to our concept of the Church as a Christian community of life.

At the same time, the light of faith also penetrates into the autonomous, self-thinking life of man. It influences our way of experiencing our situation, of judging its problems, and of forming practical plans to better our situation and solve our problems. For example, it is evident that the Christian view of man, of his vocation and eternal destiny, is the historical origin of the fundamental philosophical idea of the human person with his inviolable value and inalienable rights, which at present dominates our social and political life. Even where this idea has been divorced from faith, it remains a part of a Christian heritage. It is most probable that if Christian faith were to disappear, the personalistic idea would, in the end, lose its convincing power.

The view of man as a person is one so deeply embodied in our unconscious conviction that it not only influences the solutions we seek for our social and political problems, but even creates many of them. Some situations are unbearable and become pressing problems because we experience them in the light of a concept of the person that dominates our thought as an *idée source,* as a self-evident first principle.

We could likewise point to profound historical and theoretical connections between the Christian concept of freedom and original sin and the idea of Western democracy, between Christian eschatology and the profane idea of progress which governed our whole cultural project during the last centuries. Finally, we must also underline the fact that, just as God's word always clothed itself in human words, in the images and ideas of those to whom He addressed Himself, so will it be necessary for our growing understanding of Revelation in the Church to express itself in the categories of our own historical times. The presentation of revealed truth must of necessity follow the historical movement of our existence and our thought. In no other way will it be possible for us to understand that revealed message. Life on this earth is a perpetual development and movement. Everything that enters into this life is subject to actual earthly conditions. That which follows from the nature of things, said Newman, is a law of God's Providence. The immutability of Revelation here on earth is the immutability of growing reality which remains faithful to itself. Thus our fidelity to Revelation demands a constant translation of its imperishable content into terms that are borrowed from the contemporary expression of our self-thinking existence.

CHAPTER TWO

THOUGHT AND REALITY

1. GUIDING PRINCIPLES

The more earnestly and the longer we reflect upon conscious life, the more it appears to us as a mystery whose riches and delicate relations can never be completely expressed in our explicit thoughts and analyses. As a reproduction of lived experience, every analytical description, however refined, remains a crude simplification and a distant approximation. What we think, said Newman, is true, even at its best, only "as far as it goes." This implies that the power of human thought is far from sufficient to give adequate expression to reality. Were we to forget this and to mistake our ideas for reality itself, we would by that very fact dwell in error even if we possessed the best and most developed ideas.

With this point in mind, we notice that the most original explorers of self-conscious existence always preserved a profound and painful awareness of the distance that continually separated their analyses and the reality of life that was the object of their considerations. This realization did not diminish as they progressed in their investigations. On the contrary, they became more and more aware of that distance. Only those who borrow their ideas about life from others and do not subject them to a personal critical reflection before assimilating them, fall a prey to the illusion that they have a complete grasp of reality by means of a number of coherent concepts. This is the first principle to keep in mind when we seek an answer to the questions about the relations existing between the various aspects of our conscious existence.

The second principle concerns the unity of thought and life, which we have briefly analyzed in the previous chapter. Our life is a life that thinks itself and has to think itself if it is to maintain itself. Thinking is the proper mode of

28

human existence. Here, of course, we are not restricting the term "thought" to reflective, scientific thought; we do not even have this scientific thought primarily in mind, for the latter is a secondary form of thinking. In the first place, that which constitutes our thinking existence is spontaneous activity of self-expression in our confrontation with reality around us. This is not said to disparage the reflective, methodical forms of thinking but to assign them their proper place in the whole of thinking, because we realize that they presuppose primary experiential thinking and are related to it as methodical analyses or descriptions.

The third principle is the above-described dialectical structure of our thinking in its total movement: the to and fro between questions regarding existence which, rising from a situation, force man to think creatively and the answers that the thinking mind inscribes in that situation, thus causing new questions to arise. God's Revelation penetrates into that original dialectical movement and produces there a new dialectical dimension: a to and fro movement between the word of God, speaking from the realm of mystery and giving answers to the enigmas of our questioning existence, and the questions asked by man, who is placed before new problems because of the answers received from the realm of mystery.

2. PHASES OF SOCIAL THINKING

If we turn our attention more particularly to the Christian view about man and society, there immediately arise some questions intimately connected with the foregoing considerations. As we have mentioned, human thought, or the function of creating ideas that belong to human existence, is always directed to an interpretation of what exists or to a realization of what can or ought to exist. Thus, thought about human society is twofold: it tries, on the one hand, to explain the phenomenon of man's sociability and to penetrate to its foundation in the very being of man. On the

29

other hand, it conceives plans for ordering and reforming the concrete structures of society.

These projects are models that are considered necessary or useful structures of social existence. To realize those models in historical actuality, it is necessary to adopt definite means and techniques. Here we find ourselves in a wide domain of philosophical and theological anthropology, ethics, law, political and social action. As a being who finds himself in a definite relationship of existence to his fellow-men, man has to subject himself to definite demands in his relations with others. Certain concrete structures are best adapted to meet those demands, and in order to realize these structures, various particular means or techniques can be used.

There are, then, several phases in our thinking about the social existence of man, and these are logically connected with one another. The first phase is a consideration which, starting from the phenomenon of human life, conceives the reality of man as an ethical reality: it is proper to man to be a project, a task, for himself. This we shall have to show later on. Man is, then, something he has to realize and fulfill on his own responsibility. We use the term *"ethical reality"* to refer to man as this project. To this ethical task belongs also his attitude toward his fellow-men, in all its dimensions, including the social. Hence the ethical reality of man is socio-ethical when looked at from a certain standpoint. The starting-point of our thought concerning man's social existence is therefore an idea, an ideal of the "good man," the object of moral self-realization, self-fulfillment. This means that this kind of thinking is, from the outset, oriented to action. The good, the ideal, is by definition that which must be realized.

In the second phase a general connection is established between the ideal and human life. The idea of the good man, with respect to social existence, is then made explicit in a number of moral commandments or universal principles that must always guide the moral conduct of the community and of man as a member of the community.

In the third phase the general principles are connected with the concrete historical situation. The ethical coexistence of men does not occur in an unchangeable situation of nature, but in a historical and constantly changing cultural situation. Moreover, the changing of the socio-historical situation, the constant reform and improvement of the objective structure of society, belongs to the ethical task of human existence itself. The ideal man—the ideal humanity or ideal community—is not merely an ideal subjective mentality but also includes an ideal situation or objective structure of life, in which that mentality expresses itself and creates the conditions for its own perfect actualization.

Accordingly, the third phase of thought has a natural connection with historical and constantly changing situations. Our thinking occurs in a particular period of history. It is impossible to undo the past and to start afresh with the original condition. At its very awakening, our human existence is already determined, for good or ill, by an objective structure of life which previous generations constructed. We must make our own contribution according to the demands and the possibilities of the moment.

Those demands can be more or less urgent. Likewise, the possibilities of a creative involvement can be more or less extensive. Hence the abstract, distant ideals must be translated for our time into concrete, adapted ideals. We must make the best of the possibilities offered us by the social material at hand. To cling to beautiful abstract ideals would be to expend our thinking in useless efforts that are not directed to fulfillment. Such thinking would be utopian. It is our duty to answer the invitation of the absolute good by doing our best with what is given us, in order to realize the demands and the possibilities of our concrete situation as judged by sober practical reflection.

The fourth phase is that of the means, of political, economic and social techniques, that will enable us to realize our concretized ideals in the best way possible, in the unruly "matter" of historical humanity. This last phase, of course, postulates exact study and the manipulation of the laws that are manifested by human life in its social appearance.

This rapid analysis of the principal stages in which social thought unfolds and develops, will now enable us to determine more exactly the subject of our investigation. We will not deal with the third and fourth phases but only with the first two, which are strictly philosophical. However, since as we have seen the whole of social thought is necessarily and from the very start directed to a creative cultural task, we must deal first with some questions regarding the relation that exists between the general principles and their concrete historical realization.

3. ABSOLUTE TRUTH AND HISTORICAL RELATIVITY

The first question concerns the relation between the universal and absolute character of the insights we obtain in the first phases of social thinking and the concrete, relative character of their historical applications. The fundamental insights regarding man as a socio-ethical being and the guiding principles that follow from them, present themselves as truth, that is, as an objective revelation of the ethical man as such. They are therefore absolute and universally valid, manifesting the characteristics of an insight into truth whose validity does not depend on our will or our moods.

The guiding principles of man's cultural activity must be compelling truths. Our relative historical projects of existence must ultimately be rooted in and justified by absolute truth. If everything is relative, we have nothing to go by, nothing that can have convincing weight for man's conscience. Hence, the ultimate insights by which we determine the concrete structure of our life must impose themselves on our mind as objective truth. That which is objectively true, is true at all times and in all places. It cannot be "true this side of the Pyrenees, and false on the other."[1]

---

[1] Blaise Pascal, *Pensées,* ed. Brunschvicg, p. 294; ed. Chevalier, p. 230.

This principle must be accepted at the start. We cannot give here the complete proof of it. Moreover, such a proof would be nothing but the disclosure of an existential insight that governs life prior to all reflection. An existence that thinks and seeks itself is an existence that wants a firm grip on reality. This is evident even for a man like Ortega y Gasset, who is one of the most important modern philosophers of historical relativity. The phenomenon of thought, Ortega y Gasset holds, shows a twofold aspect: on the one hand, it manifests itself as a vital necessity for the individual and is governed by the law of subjective usefulness; on the other, the task of thought is to adjust itself to objects, and thus it stands under the objective law of truth. Since truth claims to mirror things faithfully, it owes it to itself to be one and unchangeable. As directed to objective truth and value, our spiritual activities, our understanding and willing, are vital functions whose results have a permanence and validity that are independent of life.[2]

However, it is equally clear that this absolute truth which transcends life and history is grasped by a thinking that is historical and shows all the characteristics of historical relativity. We see a clear development in man's moral self-consciousness and in his explicit consciousness of the moral good. We also observe a progressive unfolding, ramification and refinement in the most fundamental ideas that direct moral life. This development manifests two aspects. On the one hand, socio-ethical life becomes more profound, and on the other, the realm of socio-ethical knowledge becomes broader and clearer. At the beginning, the consciousness of the socio-ethical norm appears primarily in the acceptance of the common rules regulating external actions in a group. This consciousness later develops into a more interior and personal conscience that is inspired by the notion of the absolute value of human existence. From this it then follows that even the desire to do something antisocial or taking will-

---

[2]Cf. the various texts in J. H. Walgrave, *De Wijsbegeerte van Ortega y Gasset,* pp. 147-148.

ful pleasure in an imagined action, is recognized as a moral fault. It is a long way from the primitive ethics of the group that remains restricted to externals, to the ethics of mind and heart. The latter presupposes a gradual deepening and transformation of man's moral self-consciousness.

There is also noticeable a development in breadth, in the knowledge of objective moral norms. Let us simply recall the development that has led to our modern concepts of justice, which are based on a deeper understanding of equality and the inviolable rights of human persons. Who can deny that we are forced by that progress to make definite corrections and distinctions even in respect to the first principles governing the right of private property?

It is evident therefore that, although ethical truth is absolute, our thinking about that truth is subject to the law of historical development and relativity. To understand and justify this historicity and relativity, we must have recourse again to one of the fundamental guiding principles previously explained, viz., the genuine inadequacy of our concepts with respect to the total mystery that is present to the mind as an immediate experience. All thinking that is not directed to the exact analysis of phenomena presenting themselves to our senses is a clarification of a mystery in which we live and move; a mystery that is pre-given to us as a "total presence" but that can be acquired, as a conscious possession of knowledge, only through our work of thinking. This work does not create the reality of what we think, but it creates the apparatus of representations, ideas and images by means of which we appropriate that reality as a conscious possession of knowledge.

In this way then, the socio-ethical reality of our human existence is always present, though unexpressed, in our self-conscious life. This knowledge, however, can be expressed by thought and translated into a usable knowledge and insight, but only in a progressive way and in a manner never adequate and hence capable of being improved.

34

This expression and "translation" takes place in a historical way. Here we must refer to the second and third guiding principles formulated at the beginning of this chapter. In those domains of thought man moves as a whole. Thinking and living are one, they can never be separated in the concrete movement of our thinking existence. It is fallacious to imagine that the intellect, raised above life, first works out general insights for itself in a heaven of pure reason and after that applies them to life on earth. The wants and situation of changing historical life are the parents of our ideas. Life itself forces us to think, and the dialectical unfolding of life constantly obliges us to go on thinking. Or rather, thought itself is the expression of the dialectical movement manifested by our existence as an existence that thinks and seeks itself.

Expressed in terms of our schema, in and through the intellectual activities of the third and fourth phases there is also, by repercussion, a growth in the insights that belong to the domain of the first two phases. When we apply them to the evolving historical situation, the guiding principles themselves are clarified progressively in their own suprahistorical truth. The effort to understand new situations and to respond to them in the light of our socio-ethical and Christian principles does not find its terminus in making new applications of those principles. Precisely when we make such efforts, the principles themselves are not infrequently reformulated and developed, and wholesome and fundamental distinctions are brought to light. When I understand and then incorporate new facts in my life of thought, the ideas I already possessed shed a light that helps to clarify those facts. But at the same time, and by way of reaction, the facts throw a new light into my world of thought, and my thinking is clarified and enriched. In this manner our undeveloped but general insights unfold into distinct views through our distinguishing activities by way of formulations that are more differentiated.

4. "RETURN TO THE SOURCES" AND ACTUALITY

The same applies also, with due adjustment, to our knowledge of faith. Of course, the difference is great. What is clarified in our philosophical thought is the permanent, initially unexamined self-presence of our human existence. The object of faith, on the contrary, is a Revelation that became active in human history at a definite historical time as an event of salvation and that has been recorded in the inspired books of Sacred Scripture. However, that Revelation continues to work by the light of faith in the consciousness of the Church. This light of faith brings about in our minds an immediate contact with the salvific reality of which Holy Scripture and preaching bear testimony. But the explicitation of that lived faith, which is nourished by God's word and the Church, takes place again according to the laws of historical, self-thinking life. All this we have already pointed out in Chapter One. This thinking, too, remains always inadequate in comparison with the mystery that is experienced and lived by the faithful who accept it.

The development of religious thought is subject to the same historical laws as ordinary human thought. The very fact that we do not express revealed truth in heavenly words, images or ideas, but in words that borrow their meaning from earthly experience, shows for the truth of this assertion. We do not have two dictionaries, one for words that signify earthly experiences and another with the same words used as symbols of heavenly things. The meaning of our words is the one they received when they were born in man's self-thinking existence. Making an analogous use of these meanings, God speaks to us through His prophets, through Christ and the Church. The central problem of theological epistemology is precisely this: how can we speak about realities that transcend the realities of our world of experience by means of words whose meanings are insolubly connected with our earthly experience?

The particular character of Christian religious thought, when considered on the historical level, consists in a constant listening to a living, teaching authority which in turn points to a privileged period of the past: the Revelation of Christ to which the inspired Scriptures bear witness. But the dogmatic teaching authority, however much it may enjoy the guarantee of God's infallibility on the occasion of definite pronouncements, depends upon a dogmatic tradition whose clarity develops in a historical manner within the religious thought of the whole Church.

The proper rhythm of this historical religious thought is determined by a twofold movement of man's attention. The first, which is *a return to the sources (ressourcement)*, concerns itself with the historical period in which Revelation broke into history with original freshness. The second movement, namely that of *actuality,* is addressed to the present—and the present is the future in the making. The movement concerned with actuality springs from a careful attention to new questions forced upon man by contemporary situations. It results in a deeper awareness of particular aspects of dogma, leads to useful distinctions and new formulations of ancient truths according to modern ideas and terms, etc; this function is indispensable. Also it gives new life and renovation to theology. As is well-known, inbreeding leads in the end to anemia and inertia. So too, the inbreeding of concepts and views in philosophical and theological thought has a deadening effect. The constant ruminating of the same ideas, views and arguments leads to a formalism from which all genuine thinking gradually disappears. There exists also a theological pedantry. As long as we remain men, we need an awareness of being in danger; we need the stimulus offered by challenge and problems. The first and deepest tendency of life, said C. G. Jung, is sloth, the temptation to spiritual sleep. Human life can maintain itself as a creative factor only in response to the compelling challenge of what is new.

The two movements of theological interest and attention, i.e., to the sources and to the present, influence each other. It frequently happens that in the light of a new situation, the theologian discovers or rediscovers in the ancient sources of Revelation insights and ideas that did not appear, or did not show to their full advantage, in the immediate past. For example, the social needs of modern man led to the biblical rediscovery of the Church as the People of God. This interaction, after all, is in agreement with the general law of historical existence. Our memory works in the service of a creative imagination that tends to build the future. In the light of new needs and problems we discover new lessons and perspectives in the past. That is why history must be re-written from time to time.

5. The Defectiveness of Earthly Relations

The second problem in the relation between our general principles and their application in our historical existence is the defectiveness of their incarnation. "Incarnation," or "embodiment" in modern terminology, means the realization and expression of spiritual and transcendent truths and values in earthly and historical forms of life. Here it is not a question of the distance between the truth and the human words in which it is expressed but of the distance between humanly formulated insights and their active realization in the real data of historical existence. The essential points regarding this matter have already been stated above when we described the third phase of social thought. We must now go more deeply into it.

First of all, there is question here of "moral" thinking. Now, it is a general characteristic of moral thinking that a wide gap exists between the general imperatives and their concrete applications, and that this gap cannot be bridged by purely logical thinking. This assertion applies even to ordinary moral judgments, for most of the time it is not simply a matter of concluding from a general principle to a concrete case. On many occasions a concrete case falls in various respects under different imperatives which, not infrequently, conflict with one another when we are asked to make a concrete application. The various demands must be balanced against one another or sometimes they must correct one another. The final decision is then usually a more or less adulterated application of our beautiful principles. This gap between principle and application belongs to the very structure of our moral existence. The gap becomes, of course, most evident when we try to express certain ideals by means of political and social action, in the complicated and rebellious matter of modern society.

The practical virtue that enables the mind correctly to interpret a moral rule or ideal in the concrete realities of life is prudence or moral judiciousness. In this respect the classical doctrine of Aristotle and St. Thomas Aquinas stands midway between a casuistry that tries to reduce all possible cases to a definite number of patterns, and modern situation ethics that abandons all general principles and leaves moral judgments to the discretion of the individual, who must make his decisions according to circumstances on the ground of a mere general feeling or an attitude of mind.

We must accept general norms and principles. However, their application can never be automatic but always demands a personal judgment or practical wisdom (*phronesis*). Newman has given a clear expression to the personal character that is found in the original doctrine of Aristotle, in this passage from the *Grammar of Assent*: "How we are to approximate in practice to our own standard, what is right and wrong in a particular case, for the answer in fulness and accuracy to these and similar questions, the philosopher refers us to no code of laws, to no norm of moral treatise; because no science of life, applicable to the case of the individual, has been or can be written. Such is Aristotle's doctrine, and it is undoubtedly true. . . . The authoritative oracle, which is to decide our path, is something more searching and manifold than such jejune generalizations as treatises can give, which are most distinct and clear when we least need them. . . . It is a capacity sufficient for the occasion, deciding what ought to be done here and now, by this given person, under these given circumstances. . . . To learn his own duty in his own case, each individual must have recourse to his own rule."[3]

This relation between what is general and what is concrete in moral life is particularly applicable in political decisions. We must, in every situation, take account of the needs, the demands and the possibilities that are given; we must do our best to find means and enact laws that here and now reconcile in the best way the demands of the ideal and the conditions of the existing social materials. The result is always a compromise, a defective incarnation, an impure realization of the good in the present situation. In the words of Jean Lacroix: "Taking things schematically and roughly, we can distinguish three levels: the moral level, which is philosophical; the level of actual social forces, which is sociological; and the judicial level, which lies between the other two. Like the demiurg of *Timaeus,* the jurist is one who constantly strives to 'moralize' the facts more and more; with his eyes fixed on the world of moral ideas, he tries to apply to our social world the order and harmony that exists among ideas. Thus justice is neither a strongly philosophical ideal nor a purely sociological fact, but it is morality as applied to social reality."[4]

And Newman wrote: "For satisfaction, peace, liberty... were the supreme end of the law, and not mere raw justice, as such."[5] In other words, justice must be expressed in the ordering of society in such a way that the actual will, the traditions, the longings and strivings of the people and of groups of people will be satisfied and reconciled with one another in the best possible way. Otherwise politics will degenerate into an unrealism that will lead to catastrophes.

From a Christian standpoint, we must add also a practical note about the sinful selfishness of individuals and

---

[3]Newman, *Grammar of Assent,* London, 1898, pp. 354-355.

[4]Lacroix, *Itinéraire Spirituel,* (Cahiers de la Nouvelle Journée, No. 35), Paris, 1937, p. 144.

[5]Newman, "Who's to Blame?", *Discussions and Arguments,* London, 1897, p. 351.

groups that inevitably accompanies actual historical existence and is one of its intrinsic characteristics. Human existence is a sinful existence and this sinfulness is a real condition of society. Politics must take this condition into account, or rather, it cannot avoid taking it into account if it does not want to lose all effectiveness and lead to its own destruction. That sinful tendency is active in every expression of human life and determines, of course, the particular unruliness of the social matter. It is the reason why even the best political achievements are often only a shadow of our ideal projects. That is why it is only too true that even those who are led by the purest intentions, not infrequently sully their hands when they venture into the political arena. This is undoubtedly one of the severest trials that a Christian politician is called to undergo.

The bitter criticisms of Pascal retain a certain amount of truth: man has a natural feeling for justice but he is unable to grasp it and express it in his laws. The truth lies somewhere in the middle: we are able and we are not able, that is, we are able to realize the good but only in a deficient way. However, we must look upon the little good that we do, even when it is still far removed from our desired ideals, as a forward step in the gradual and laborious ascent of history. As Christians, we have a special reason for hope and courage. We know that evil results from sin and that it is not fatally anchored in man's essence. We believe that a remedy against sin is at work in history and that salvation through Christ will encompass the whole of life.

CHAPTER THREE

CULTURE AND GRACE

1. HUMANISM, MYSTICISM OR ESCHATOLOGY?

Regarding the relation between our Christian view of man and our historical task of developing the earthly community according to a moral idea, there is one problem that requires a separate treatment. The good of salvation, the life of grace, is not of this world. It is a communion of life with God through Jesus Christ. Those who together share that communion with God are also in communion with one another. The spiritual atmosphere of that community is faith, the bond is charity that unites us in the friendship of God and therefore also, in God, is directed to all those who are invited to the same friendship by God's love. That community of grace with God is the "kingdom of God" or the "kingdom of heaven." As realized in Christ, it is also called the "Mystical Body of Our Lord." Its earthly expression, its social incarnation in our world, is the Church: a visible, hierarchically constituted society, whose social symbolic acts of worship, the sacraments, cultivate and foster the growth of the invisible community of those who share in it with faith and with the necessary religious commitment.

The Church is truly an earthly society in which the community of the heavenly kingdom of God is realized, and the risen Christ is the *Kyrios,* the Lord and King of that society. Nevertheless, in St. John's Gospel, which is the Gospel of His Kingdom, Christ Himself says: "My Kingdom is not of this world" (John 18:36).

If the concept of community according to Christian Revelation refers only to a heavenly and divine kingdom that does not belong to this world, although it is prepared here "in a mystery" and is already present and operative; if the salvation preached by Christianity is not a part of history but by nature transcends it—then there is no escaping the question of what relation exists between that revealed reality which we grasp in grace and the cultural task within our world that is given to man as a project belonging to his very nature. Does not Christ precisely ask us to turn our attention away from the "world," built by sinful forces, and keep our eyes on heaven, where our life even now is "hidden with Christ in God"? Is it not demanded of us that we should forget earthly cares and seek only "the kingdom of God and His justice?" Or, on the contrary, does the active presence of God's kingdom among us demand rather that we become involved with a new spirit in our historical social task? In other words, what is the relation between the heavenly kingdom of God, the substance of the Christian Revelation, and the earthly kingdom of man that is the purpose of the immanent tendency of human existence and history?

Questions like these bring to the fore the whole problem of Christian humanism: a problem that is not undisputed in Catholic thought. It was in line with this that the Archbishop of Paris said at the close of the *Semaine des Intellectuels Catholiques* in 1950: "Is it possible for me to be a Christian and at the same time continue to love the world? Must I renounce culture in order to become a saint? Am I faithful to God if I am faithful to man?... The solutions that are proposed in regard to the relation between humanism and grace are sometimes diametrically opposed to each other.... Everywhere and on every occasion I notice how in our country, as elsewhere in the Church, there grow up two spiritual families that stand juxtaposed or even opposed to each other. On one side is the group which we can call the "mystics," on the other, "the humanists."[1]

Others dislike the idea of opposing to an earthly kingdom of man a divine kingdom which, like a bridgehead in a foreign territory, has been established on the other side of eternity by the heavenly "bridgebuilder" (*pontifex*). They prefer to speak of a divine kingdom that was foretold

---

[1] *L'Humanisme et la grâce. Semaine des Intellectuels Catholiques* (May 7-14, 1950), Paris, 1950, pp. 209-210.

by Christ and for which we are still waiting with constant longing and nostalgia. The kingdom is then not so much an eternal kingdom that descends vertically, as it were, into our earthly history, but it is an ultimate kingdom that will be inaugurated at Christ's second coming and that, in contrast with the horizontal course of time, will close earthly history and replace it. The Church is then like Noah's Ark, floating on the waves of perdition, in which redeemed mankind waits for a new beginning and prays in accordance with Christ's teaching: "Thy kingdom come."

In this way, a humanistic Christianity is opposed to an eschatological Christianity.

2. THE CHURCH, KINGDOM OF HEAVEN AND ULTIMATE KINGDOM

There should not be any essential disagreement in respect to these problems, for the dispute rests upon false dilemmas. If those opposite views are considered within an all-embracing vision, they are automatically resolved into living and inspiring tensions. We shall examine this question from the biblical-theologian standpoint in the next chapter. First, however, it seems opportune to develop a fundamental and systematic position.

Without having recourse to exegetical proof, we think we are justified in saying that the kingdom of heaven preached by Christ is both supernatural and earthly, historical and eschatological. It is the true incarnation of the heavenly community into an earthly community, just as Christ is the true incarnation of God in a historical figure. But that divine kingdom on earth is still hidden in historical mankind with respect to its inmost nature, just as Christ's divinity was hidden when He dwelled amongst us "in the form of a servant." It is present and active "as a mystery."

The divine kingdom on earth is subject to the earthly conditions of existence of sinful mankind. It does not yet manifest itself in the form of existence that was inaugurated by Christ's Resurrection. The glorious character of the

44

Church is not yet manifest; it is not yet revealed; it does not yet shine through the Church's outward appearance. Her glorious existence will come about only at the end of the time when the identity of God's earthly kingdom and of His heavenly kingdom will appear plainly, when God's will shall be done "on earth as it is in heaven" and the humble appearance will be transformed into glory. Thus the Church stands in a vertical tension toward the eternal kingdom of heaven and, at the same time, in a horizontal tension toward the coming ultimate kingdom. This twofold tension is visible in all her dimensions.

Accordingly, the question is whether or not the Christian view of life invites us to live in heaven above the earthly, to look toward the future kingdom transcending history, in such a way that we must look upon man's original task of realizing an earthly cultural society as something that is unimportant or abrogated.

3. CULTURE AS THE EXERCISE OF HUMAN EXISTENCE

In reply to that question one could simply point out that culture, concerning which man allegedly must choose pro or con, is nothing but man himself; it is man in the essential exercise of his manhood. Man is not a kind of princely being who, accomplished in his manhood by nature, has the choice of committing himself to culture or not. Man enters into this world and is present in it through his body as a being of pure potentiality.

Everything human is a spiritual acquisition in and through the body and the material world. Nothing that is human can be something that is given by nature; everything is a task, a vocation, an acquisition. This self-realization of man in the world is called "culture." The great domains of culture are the principal aspects of a humanity that unfolds and develops through self-realization. To maintain that something has descended from heaven to earth and now obliges man to choose for or against culture, is like declaring that something has penetrated into manhood to stop man from being man.

We do not deny that the core of man's being, the spiritual principle of his personality, can have another mode of existence than that of his earthly bodily being. But the way man actually exists on earth is as a freedom that can realize itself in this world only through bodily activity. Such an existence is a form of being and life that develops itself in its own way. This self-creating activity together with its objective results we call "culture."

4. THE EARTHLY BODILY CHARACTER OF THE KINGDOM OF HEAVEN

It must be kept in mind that, as we have shown in Chapter One, a divine Revelation can be known only within a life that realizes itself through thinking. No matter how much grace may cure the heart of man and open it to God's Revelation, His word can be apprehended only as an answer to a life that questioningly tries to understand itself. No matter how much grace awakens our human answer to Revelation, this answer can be given only in terms of human life. And this life forms a whole: "man moves as a whole."

In this historical life of humanity that develops itself through culture, the kingdom of heaven has descended. It has incarnated itself in the structures of that historical life. For Revelation was expressed in human words that were formed and given a meaning by culture. Theological thinking uses the acquisitions of our natural thought to clarify and explain the data of our faith. The sacramental liturgy uses a symbolism which we are now able to understand as expressive of grace because we had first learned to understand it as a natural symbolism.

All the forms in which the sacramental economy of salvation is expressed were originally imploring rites of a natural religion, but now they are filled with a heavenly answer of salvation. Worship in which powerless prayer addressed itself to God was transfigured by God into a worship in which He imparts to us His salvific power. The liturgy, making use of all the means provided by human art, has created a grandiose world of Christian symbols. The Church, too, in her administration and guidance makes use of forms of organization, legislation, judicial pronouncements, diplomatic relations, etc., that were formed by human culture. Without all these aspects of ecclesiastical incarnation it is simply impossible for the divine kingdom to exist in the historical world.

The Church is the kingdom of God realized in a body of human culture. The kingdom unfolds itself in historical forms that were devised by man. And through this incarnation it is also involved in and committed to the variability of our existence with its constant creation of new forms. It must also march forward with the inevitable movement and metamorphoses of history. Hence it cannot at a particular moment gratefully borrow some forms and then refuse to be involved in all further development. If the Church wishes to continue to exist according to the laws of earthly existence—and it is evident that God has not made any exceptions in that regard—she must also remain present in the whole development of culture, grow with it and constantly retranslate herself into modern forms. If she fails to do this, the body of the ecclesial incarnation will gradually become divorced from the living environment by which it was originally fashioned and by which it must continue to be nourished. In that case the Church will become estranged from the world and Revelation will finally lose all contact with living humanity.

That is why another possibility imposes itself on our minds, namely, that God's kingdom, involved in culture because of its incarnation, permeates that culture from within its spirit and directs its development instead of being carried away by that culture's natural development. Nothing is able to arrest the course of history. History is man in action, man in the exercise of manhood. If Christianity

47

does not want to be bypassed in that creative movement of culture, if it refuses to be left behind as archaic, it must be present and active in that movement and function in it as an inspiring principle.

According to the most evident historical laws, it is necessary to declare that if the Church does not want to pine away and die in her historical embodiment—and hence disappear from our world—she must engage in the task of adapting the human material from which her body is fashioned, to the demands of her spirit. This justification of Christian culture, as a function of the kingdom of God that establishes itself in historical mankind, is something that cannot be denied. In this domain especially lies the great task the layman must fulfill in the social body of Christians. For laymen, as actively involved in all those fields of culture, have as their task the Christianization of those domains, that is, to influence their development in a Christian way.

Hence, it follows from the very nature of things that the kingdom of God cannot possibly establish itself in the forms of life man has on earth and subsequently demand that its members renounce that same life from which it borrows the forms that make possible its existence in this world. "No one ever hated his own flesh" said St. Paul (Eph. 5:29). How, then, could the Church ask Christians to be indifferent toward something on which her very existence in this world depends? God's heavenly kingdom did not come down into the earthly kingdom of man in order to take its place or repress it, but to save it. Man is precisely the being who realizes himself through culture. This is his dynamic definition. The salvation of man must therefore mean also the salvation of culture. The whole man is saved, not merely a soul that dwells within him and that does not belong to the world. "To save" does not mean to break up or to injure things, but to create a peace that is all-embracing and making all things whole. Holiness is not division but wholeness. Adam is not abolished in Christ but is renewed in Him; he is "recapitulated," says St. Irenaeus. The cultural task, which undoubtedly was entrusted to Adam according to *Genesis,* is renewed in a higher task within the history of salvation.

5. NATURE AND GRACE

We can now synthetically develop the various aspects of the Christian-humanistic idea in the form of a commentary on the famous Thomistic adage: "Grace does not destroy nature, but presupposes, perfects and elevates it." Both terms of the comparison are sufficiently clear in the light of what we have said thus far. The nature in question is human nature, that is, the original phenomenon of being-man, a being that realizes itself and creates history by means of that self-realization.

Thus the domain of our nature is the domain of our autonomous freedom. Grace is a new dimension of being which through a new creation of God is called up in man and, at the same time, completely transforms our original, autonomous manhood. This new life can be acquired only as a gratuitous and unmerited gift; it cannot be won by any cultural effort. It remains a grace, a gratuitous gift, because it is a way of being whose proper action consists in a personal communion with God Himself. Now, a personal communion is necessarily a gift made by the other. That personal communion with God is already a reality on earth through "charity," but it is still hidden in the mystery of life of faith. It will be completed only in the heavenly communion with the unhidden Godhead.

6. GRACE DOES NOT DESTROY NATURE

God's wise and loving plan of creation is sufficient to encompass in their unimpaired entirety all the diverse orders of creatures: the order of nature with its laws of normal evolution; the order of human freedom with its dialectical historicity; the order of grace as directed to eternity and to the final event. The ultimate aim to which that whole orderly plan of creation is directed is that of grace. There is only one plan of creation; no additions or later changes were necessary in the plan God had first made. Nature exists for the sake of culture and culture for the sake of grace. Nature realizes its meaning when it is taken up into the life of freedom, and the life of freedom attains its purpose when taken up into the life of grace.

This transition from the one level to another does not signify that the lower order is destroyed or diminished. By being what it is, every partial order of creation makes its own contribution to the meaningful realization of the whole. "To be" is to work. Activity is the exercise of existence. This means that, within God's single plan of creation and salvation, nature is to make its contribution to the realization of the whole in accordance with the laws of evolution; incarnate freedom will be directed to the same end by achieving culture in nature; and grace will reach the end itself by appealing to man in the exercise of his freedom and by directing him, even in his earthly existence, to the goal that lies beyond, to eternal communion with God. In this way salvation, God's work of making man holy, aims at "wholeness," it is the bringing to completion of unimpaired parts in the all-embracing realization of the ultimate end.

7. GRACE PRESUPPOSES NATURE

This statement determines more fully a particular aspect of the relation between man's earthly self-fulfillment and his being-fulfilled by God's grace. The success of God's kingdom on earth depends in a certain sense on the success of the kingdom of man. The ordering of culture is like a "material disposition" for the incarnation of the kingdom of God in the historic life of man. This kingdom, insofar as it is actualized on earth, can exist and flower only in the historical forms of self-making life. Hence, it must incorporate that form-giving activity of culture into its own task and transform culture into a body that shares in the animating life of grace. This we have already shown above.

This second principle implies that we must properly define the manner in which man's spiritual self-realization cooperates in the realization of divine grace in man. At once there must be excluded any idea that man would be able to acquire, by means of autonomous culture, the slightest participation in the good of salvation which is God Himself. Every acquisition in the order of salvation is the work of grace and a gift of God. Nor can man indirectly draw grace to himself by creating in himself and by his own efforts a positive disposition for grace. Everything that actively prepares us and directs us to grace, comes from grace. The idea that man by himself and, as it were, independently of grace can do something that has salvific power, must be entirely rejected. But man's answer, which God's call of grace evokes, is given by man in the style and with the riches of his own developed personality. For example, the conversion and holiness of a St. Augustine bear the evident marks of his cultivated humanity.

Grace is life, divine life, but it is a life that lets its fruitfulness mature in human forms. Grace is not an impersonal treasure of pure "being" in the core of the soul. It constitutes a personal possession that tends to unfold itself in personal activity, at least in a human being who has reached a sufficient level of personal life. Being, says St. Thomas, is for action. Activity is the exercise, the realization, of being. Grace realizes its being in our action according to the style and the possibilities of our personality.

Of course, God can produce even in the simplest souls a most perfect form of love, which is the essence and the measure of holiness. In such a case the appearance of love will, as in St. Bernadette, radiate the charm of an unartificial spontaneity. However, it must not be forgotten that Bernadette's humanity was also a product of culture. When we hear the word "culture," we too readily associate it with the idea of an intellectual and artistic civilization which appears to us as something artificial and complex rather than spontaneous. Nevertheless, the heart of culture, the great fruit of self-thinking and self-making life, lies in the inner order and unification of our being under the direction of a moral value. The more simple this value, the more perfect it will be. Pure human nature, however, is not simple. It is "wild," that is, scattered and divided in the plurality and unsteadiness of passional mobility. This we shall have to show further on. True simplicity is culture. However wonderful the help given by grace to accomplish simplicity and singleness of purpose, these are not attained without an inner self-control that is in reality a work of culture under the impetus of grace. Both the figure of simple charm that we behold in an unartificial human being like St. Bernadette, untouched by any intellectual development or reflectivity, and the figure of polished self-control admirable in an intellectual like St. Francis de Sales, are products of culture under the inspiration of grace.

In sum, grace is life. This life unfolds itself on earth in human forms. The style and the riches of those forms of life are results of human self-culture even in the case of works of grace.

When we apply this same idea to the social domain, we must call attention to the fact that if the social problems are not solved in a Christian spirit, they will inevitably be solved in a spirit that is in opposition to Christianity. Mankind then becomes more and more estranged from Christianity by the influence of its social environment, so that the kingdom of God loses its incarnation in earthly, historical reality. The whole tragedy of socialism in our Western culture serves to remind us of this truth.

The social patterns of our life are not determined by natural instinct as is the case with bees and ants. We ourselves form those patterns according to the circumstances and in accord with the plans that we have conceived. This activity takes place in a particular attitude of mind. This attitude, however, does not remain purely spiritual but expresses itself in the concrete social structure which it creates. Because man is a spirit who develops and reveals himself in matter through his body, everything that man calls forth in the world is the incarnation of a particular spiritual attitude or conviction. It is evident, however, that the pride and selfishness of individuals and groups constantly turn our world into a milieu of disorder and division. In such an environment men are not only bodily exposed to the unspeakable misery of hot and cold wars, of oppression and persecution, of injustice and tyranny, but they are also abandoned to barbarous influences that coarsen and harden their souls so that "love" becomes a mere word and Christ's message sounds like unreal sentimentality.

When the activities of philosophical and scientific thought, of literature and art are inspired by a certain spirit, they bring forth cultural products that change man's living environment into a realm where the consciousness of God is obscured. In such a milieu man feels more and more closed off from the transcendent. God is silent, God is absent, because the world's forms of thought interpose themselves like a separating screen between God and the human mind. It becomes then increasingly difficult for man to discover and hear God's Revelation.

There are also certain social structures that turn the human world into a hell of temptations, a spiritual morass in which men gradually sink away. In such an environment man is prevented from rising to the level of a moral personality and fulfilling his Christian vocation.

Against that constant paganizing transformation of the environment by those who follow Adam in his pride, stands the vocation of Christianizing the environment addressed to people willing to follow Christ in His service of love. The work of the Christian statesman who desires to regulate national and international relations in a spirit of peace, justice and freedom; the work of the Christian thinker and artist by which the tarnished and darkened world recovers its spiritual lustre and transparency; the struggle of the Christian social worker and educator to make the environment wholesome, the formation of good human relations and attitudes; and the establishment of institutions that foster the good and help men in their endeavor to develop a harmonious personality—all these Christian cultural activities are not irrelevant to God's kingdom on earth. They collaborate in the building of the kingdom.

The social conditions of life, the political order, the cultural climate, the general mentality, all the concrete realities of our earthly, historical existence can be suitable or unsuitable for the reception of the gospel seed and for letting it reach mature fruitfulness. Taking humanity as it actually is, every effective apostolate presupposes two kinds of activities, namely, those that are directly concerned with salvation and others that prepare the environment. It is not sufficient to scatter the seed, the field must be cleared and cultivated. It is not sufficient to add leaven to the dough, but the dough must also be properly kneaded.

Christian cultural work in the world is a struggle. In the Sacrament of Confirmation we are publicly authorized and marked in our souls to make that struggle a form of worship of God.

8. GRACE PERFECTS NATURE

This theological maxim expresses the precise relation between human culture and the kingdom of God from the opposite direction. The growth of the kingdom of God on earth in a certain sense presupposes the flourishing condition of the kingdom of man; but at the same time, the successful achievement of man's cultural task in the concrete conditions of earthly existence presupposes the healing and helping influence of grace. Even if we abstract from the Christian interpretation of the Fall of man, one can clearly see that in man's earthly existence as a self-thinking and self-making being there are at work not only forces that help him develop culture but also inimical forces tending to destroy its achievements. Both arise from the same mysterious source—the freedom of man.

In his historical analysis of the downfall of Greece, Thucydides puts his finger exactly on the deepest wound of mankind. The fall of Greece, he tells us, is to be attributed to *arche,* that is, the lust for power. This lust, in Hellas, prompted an insane struggle for power and control between city and city, between party and party in the same city, between leader and leader within the same party. *Arche* is called "pride" in Christian terminology, for pride is, according to St. Thomas, an unruly desire to have power over others while retaining one's own perfect independence. In Sartre's existentialism that tendency is the deepest passion of human existence, the absurd desire for absolute freedom. This proud tendency is a demonic force that constantly pulls down and destroys the graceful building of culture. Pride can be both collective or individual. The pride of the "we," which is the pride of the weak, is as bad as the pride of the "I," which is the pride of the strong. Collective pride is even more enduring and more disastrous. It hides easily behind a mask of individual humility and unselfish service to a good cause.

According to the Christian analysis, that all-pervasive and all-disturbing tendency of man is not, as Sartre seems to think, the existential act of being-man as such; but it is a degeneration coming from original sin. It can be healed by grace. That is why Chesterton said that the joyful message of Christianity is the message of original sin. For the Christian interpretation delivers us from the oppressive Sartrian delusion that pride is an absurdity belonging to the very essence of man. The Christian interpretation makes us understand that that absurdity has entered our existence through human freedom, and thus prepares us for the message that Christ's power dwells in this world and is able to cure that evil in its very roots.

"Our grandfathers, in their simplicity, found it hard, if not impossible, to believe in Original Sin; it is not so with us; perhaps alone among the traditional dogmas this can now be accepted as almost self-evident."[2] Contemporary thinking concerning historical culture is obsessed by the idea of original sin. Everyone has his own version or interpretation, but most

[2]A. G. Smith, *The Western Dilemma,* London, 1954, pp. 110-111.

thinkers agree that historical mankind seems to suffer from a mysterious evil that will prove fatal unless remedy is found.

In a famous article about the significance of Jesus Christ, Gandhi said that, considering the world with its cruelty, its tyranny, its injustice and hypocrisy, he was inclined to despair of the possibility of restoring mankind. But, he continued, I have new hope when I think of Christ. For in Christ the possibility of a restoring love has been manifested in its most perfect purity. From the Christian viewpoint, Christ is not only a historical example but an ever living Savior who, through His sorrowful sacrifice, has entered into the glory of the Resurrection. "Foreordained Son of God by an act of power (Rom. 1:4), He is always present among us and gives us of His Spirit in order to deliver our "crooked love" from enslavement to the "I" and to unite us in peace and harmony with God, with our fellow-man and with the whole of creation.

If pride is a demonic force that constantly breaks down the historical realizations of mankind, grace is the divine healing power which casts out devils and can extirpate the disease that afflicts human culture. We must add that grace is also the most powerful help for the development of our interior personal culture from which social harmony springs. For peace with oneself is the source of peace with others. The Christian's moral self-training is integrated into the finality of grace from which it receives its most powerful motivation. Christian self-training in self-control under the impetus of grace.

9. Grace Elevates Nature

In this maxim the most fundamental relation between manhood and grace finds expression. There is a real, inner continuity between man's self-making existence and the new existence added to it by God's grace. The term "added," however, is a provisional expression, for it could imply an erroneous idea. As self-making our existence is integrated into the new life that God cultivates in us. Adam is repeated, so to speak, in Christ but in a more sublime way. This means an elevation, not an abolition nor a mere addition. Our autonomous endeavors for personal wholeness that are impeded by sinfulness are successfully repeated in the wholeness which God's grace operates in us. But this second fulfillment, however unmerited and supernatural it may be, is the completion of the first. Grace does not add anything that is foreign to our manhood. On the contrary, our manhood is interiorly completed thereby. With grace I am not "man plus something else" but I am completely and perfectly man. Were an animal to receive human life and the ability to think, it would cease to be an animal. In other words, its animal nature would be destroyed by that "grace." But when we, men, are made partakers of God's life in communion with Him we do not cease to be men. We are not thereby less men, but more so. The divinized man is the true man: "Grace does not destroy nature but elevates it."

This relation of inner continuity is inscribed in the depths of our humanity. Our thinking existence as a self-seeking existence discovers itself as seeking God, as seeking Him in His unconcealedness. Being-man is question and quest for God Himself. Hence Christian Revelation is also a reply to a question that animates the whole of culture, even when a culture does not acknowledge it or unconsciously rejects it. It is in this sense that we must understand the famous and often discussed statement of St. Thomas that man by nature desires to contemplate God in his unveiled essence.

The whole spiritual movement of our questioning and seeking existence is by its very nature hiddenly directed to communion with God. For only in Him can man find his life's fulfillment and happiness. Where man in his thinking strives for truth, he unconsciously aims at an absolute Truth which he is unable to grasp by any effort of thought because that truth is the inner hiddenness of God which can be known only when He comes out of His concealedness. Where man attempts in his creative art to reveal through beauty the hidden truth of things, he always aims at an ultimate mystery which he cannot make transparent in any form because that secret is the inner mystery of the wholly Transcendent God. Where man proceeds in his moral action toward the realization of the good, he is drawn by the absolute Good, the communion with God Himself which cannot be won nor merited by any created being because He is a Person; and communion with Him can only be the free gift of His love creating this communion. When man in his ascent to culture arrives at the limits of his possibilities, he is not yet at the limit of the craving that unconsciously inspires all his endeavors. The acquired humanness of culture asks in its own line for the freely given humanness of grace.

That inner continuity, by which grace fulfills the deepest longings dwelling in the heart of culture, does not do away with the real supernatural character of grace. For "supernatural" means, according to the classical definition, "that which surpasses the active powers (the culture) and the demands of all created nature." In this sense God, as object of a community life, is essentially supernatural. He is the Transcendent, the completely Other. He has indeed displayed a likeness of His Being in creation, but it is so infinitely distant a likeness that it merely points to His existence and only allows us to say that the proper mode of the existence of His infinite perfection cannot be expressed by any creative image.

God is "The Mystery," and this mystery is a Person, be it in a totally different sense than the persons that we know from experience. Of course, the personal character of the Creator is such that between Himself and others there cannot be that sort of opposition which marks the relation between created persons. The absolute fullness of Infinite Being cannot oppose itself as a closed interiority to any other being, for this would make It limited and finite. However transcendent and irreducible He is to His creatures, the Creator permeates them totally and constantly, for they exist only insofar as they are receiving their whole being from Him. He is *intimior intimo meo* (St. Augustine), more intimately present in me and in all things and persons than I am in myself. But if the proper characteristic of personality is self-possession of one's own being, as we shall argue further on, then of course an infinite and absolute being must be eminently personal. To deny this would be to degrade the divine to the realm of infra-personal existence, to something which, like mere matter, is always and totally out of itself.

God, then, is a person, but His created works do not reveal to us His inner life in the way actions of our fellow-men reveal their inner lives. Man as a subject who objectivates himself in his bodily appearance and his works gives us an approach to his interior by means of outward expressions, although even in his case real personal communion requires that he freely reveal himself in the encounter. God, however, is a pure subject. Nothing created gives access to His inner "Mystery." It is possible to know Him only in a communion of life in which He reveals Himself, makes Himself known, to the unmerited happiness of the elect.

The fundamental thesis that expresses the intimate unity of our manhood and our being a child of God through grace, has been the occasion of endless discussions and much misunderstanding. It is possible to explain this unity in various ways, but it must never be done so as to suggest that grace is something strange, something unexpected, that, coming from outside, seems to be added to our original manhood. The thesis of the "supernatural veneer" (*surnaturel plaqué*) is a theological schizophrenia which, in our culture, has fostered the disastrous separation between an increasingly unreal Christianity and an increasingly profane civilization. The question concerning our communion with God is and remains, according to the title of a book by Father Brocardus Meijer, "the first question of life."[3]

---

[3] Br. Meijer, *De eerste levensvraag,* Roermond, 1940.

Thus it becomes clear that the whole tendency of culture in its integral, original movement is not opposed to the movement of grace nor simply juxtaposed to it, but that it asks for grace and goes forward to it. The dilemma is not "either culture or grace," but "either sinful culture or grace." We are not asked to choose between humanism and Christianity, but between an open and a closed humanism. Just as our awareness of our sinful perdition opens us to the revelation of salvation, so does the full comprehension of our original movement toward complete manhood open our mind to the revelation of the Christian vocation. Is it not precisely the meaning of culture that it should make us realize more and more, in the course of the progressive fulfillment of its possibilities, that the spiritual tendency which has goaded us along the way to culture also prompts our questioning and quest for the gift of God's communion, and that our heart's unrest can find rest only in God? This original meaning of creative culture must be increasingly experienced and appreciated in the work of Christian civilization.

10. CHRIST THE KING

We may say in conclusion that not merely some part or some aspect of culture is taken up in the order of supernatural life, but the entire culture with all its spiritual and material objectives, all its structures and techniques. Nothing is foreign to Christ except sin, which must be overcome by His grace. Everything takes part in salvation because salvation signifies the wholeness of holiness and leaves out nothing except evil which is always divisive.

With respect to society, then, it follows that political, economic and social activities with their diverse aims, their structures and techniques, their skills and capabilities, become a service, a worship offered to the God of salvation. If the kingdom of heaven is truly among us, if the power of the kingdom is at work in us, we must direct our efforts to the construction of earthly life according to the model of the heavenly Jerusalem that descends from heaven and in which our earthly community is taken up and will be transformed.

This worship rendered by the whole of earthly life is wonderfully expressed in the feast of Christ the King. Its fundamental idea is precisely that Christ is not only the king of a spiritual kingdom but that, since the Resurrection, His kingdom has been victoriously established in the earthly kingdom and completely encompasses the latter. That is why we pray that everything may become subject to His gentle rule and that, assisted by His grace, we may make of the kingdom of this earth a "kingdom of justice, love and peace." The feast of Christ the King is the feast of Christian social humanism.

CHAPTER FOUR

THE EARTHLY COMMUNITY IN THE BIBLE

1. Introductory Remarks

Before explaining Christianity's social view it is necessary to recall a few principles that were mentioned in Chapter One. A view is Christian insofar as it accepts Christian Revelation as a norm of truth. However, Revelation was not intended to give us a developed doctrine about earthly man and his social existence. Revelation is concerned with man's relation to God, his Savior. Nevertheless, Revelation sheds much light upon man and his earthly social relations. For Revelation is an answer to questions that arise in man's life, just as Revelation is also expressed in terms and concepts that have been formed by man's historical life. Hence the Christian view of man is the result of the Christians' life here upon earth insofar as that life is self-thinking and self-making in communion with the whole of historical mankind, but in the light and according to the norm of God's word.

A methodical analysis of the Christian social view requires, therefore, a twofold examination. The first is a biblico-theological one. It assembles and synthesizes the various elements found in the inspired documents of salvation history. The second examination, as we shall explain and show below, belongs rather to Christian philosophy. In it we shall attempt to construct a synthesis of a modern view of society that is the result of Christian thinking about life as it, at this historical moment, manifests itself and asks for clarification. Reserving this second inquiry for following chapters, we will address ourselves here to Scripture.

2. Greece and Israel

According to the most widely accepted schema, the one which dominates the historical view of Western culture, our civilization is the synthesis of a religion that originated in Israel and a humanism that is the fruit of Greek thought. This schema, however, is misleading. No doubt, Greek thought made an important contribution to the formation of Western humanism. Rationality came to life in Greek thought in the sense that the Greeks posited the idea that man must live according to his reason. And precisely this rationality was destined to become one of the most important tools in the construction of Western humanism. Yet it remained only a means.

The rationality of Greco-Roman culture remained imprisoned in a world-view which, seen as a whole, was anti-historical and hence, to that extent, also anti-humanistic. It remained always a general postulate in Greek thought that the material world is a world of eternal motion. This motion is ruled by an inevitable necessity from which human life here below cannot escape. The great cosmic year, a world-cycle determined by the course of the planets, is constantly repeated. It begins with a "golden age" and thereafter life declines in ever diminishing power. History is not an ascent but an inevitable decadence. At the end comes the destruction of the world by fire (*ekpurosis*) and from it the world is reborn for a new cycle of life.

This vision we find in Heraclitus and in the later works of Plato. Through the Stoics and Neo-Pythagoreans it became the dominant world-view of the Greco-Roman empire: "There came a moment when the motives of the 'eternal return' and the 'end of the world' dominate the whole of Greco-Roman culture."[1] It led to philosophical views which "betray a very strong anti-historical attitude and a determination to defend oneself against history."[2] Such an attitude was evidently anti-humanistic. What man accomplishes in the course of his earthly existence was not regarded as an autonomous progress, but as a mere factor in a gen-

---

[1]Mircea Eliade, *Der Mythos der ewigen Wiederkehr*, Düsseldorf, 1953, p. 178.
[2]*Ibid*, p. 179.

eral movement leading to inevitable decadence. There was no room here for an end (*telos*), for an ideal within history that could be pursued successfully by the efforts of human culture. Thus in Neo-Pythagoreanism, in the Gnosis and the mystery cults, salvation was always some form of escape from the prison of earthly existence. The severe rationality of the Stoic, on the other hand, has at most only an inner acceptance and a practical following of the cosmic reason or necessity to which all things and man also were subject.

While it may be true, then, that Hellas has given us an important spiritual instrument for the development of humanism, the world-view within which such a humanism was able to develop did not come from Hellas but from Israel. In Israel man penetrated into the open space of history: a history that is led by God to a *telos,* to a crowning end, and in which God has given to man, endowed with mind and freedom, a definite earthly task.

3. INDIA AND PALESTINE

It is necessary for us to take a wider view of the world in which the humanism of Israel arose. The data gathered today by the comparative history of religions and cultures force us to distinguish between two radically different views regarding the place and meaning of man within the all-embracing mystery of reality. These two divergent fundamental ideas about existence divide civilized humanity into two spiritual hemispheres. The historical source of the first lies in Palestine, the second arose in India; and the roots of both plunge equally deep into the distant past. The first spiritual hemisphere now embraces especially the worlds of Christianity and Islam. Hinduism and Buddhism belong to the second hemisphere.

Let us begin with the second. We find here a fundamental distinction between two levels of existence: the level of that which is "unborn, non-become, non-made, uncompounded," and the level of "what is born, has become, is made, is compounded." These are the very terms attributed to Buddha.[3] Both levels are eternal. Above is the world of immovable eternity, below the world of the eternal return. The latter sprang in one way or another from the first. The nature of this world and its relation to the eternal world are not very clear but subject to various interpretations.

The human person (*purusha*) belongs by his very nature to the higher world. But, on account of some mysterious metaphysical accident, man has become a prisoner, as an individual and limited conscious being, in the world of birth, plurality and composition. In this world the person is estranged from himself and covered, as it were, with a veil. His existence in this world is suffering. By the law of his deeds (*karma*) the person is bound to the wheel of rebirth. Salvation consists in escaping from the insane earthly life. By training and meditation a person can break the bonds that attach him to the world of his birth and death and can re-discover his pure being in the world of the unborn. Various interpretations are offered in respect to the constitution of the ultimate end. Buddha always refused to say anything about it. He was satisfied with the four noble truths: this is suffering; this is the cause of suffering; this is the end of suffering; this is the way to the end of suffering. But what the blessed ultimate end actually is men will know when they attain salvation.

Eastern thought, even when it seems to express a strict monism (the unity of the all), is always characterized by the fundamental dualism of two levels of existence. In the spiritual world of India, the religious concern is in the first place not God but the soul, the person and his liberation. The problem of God, according to Buddha, is not even to the point for those who are on earth. For the Hindu, man is the divine or at least a part of it; the divine is the core,

---

[3] *Udana,* 81, quoted by E. Conze, *Buddhist Texts Through the Ages,* Oxford, 1954, p. 95.

the very nature of man, and it is his task, by means of exercise, to attain to a state of consciousness in which that divine, now free from self-estrangement, finds again its pure self.

It is obvious that in such a view the world of birth and plurality offers no room for history. Hinduism and Buddhism are anti-historical and radically anti-humanistic. There can never be a question of realizing a meaning or value within the movement of earthly existence. This existence is utterly meaningless: an eternal, senseless repetition. There can be question of man's self-realization only in the sense of a liberation from the world of meaninglessness.

Against that conception stands another view whose principal source lies in Palestine. It is characteristic of Judaism, Christianity and Islam. We shall not speak about Islam, the last great branch that arose within the development of the Israelitic view, but we shall confine ourselves to the line of development that can be followed in the books of the Old and New Testaments.

Let us remark in passing that the two spiritual hemispheres which we have opposed above were not entirely closed to each other. In our civilization the fundamental conception of Pythagoreanism, Platonism and the world of Gnosticism bears a strong likeness to the world of India. The historical relation between Indian and Greek thought, however, is still insufficiently explored. Platonism has also exercised a strong influence on Christian thought. On the other hand, the Bhakti religion of India manifests a certain resemblance with our own world of thought. But here also no satisfactory explanation has yet been given of possible historical influences. In any case, both Islam and Christianity have exercised a strong influence in later developments of Hinduism.

4. THE HEBREW VIEW OF MAN

The Hebrew view of man is fundamentally different from the Greco-Platonic outlook or that of India. It is closely connected with the Hebrew idea of the divine. The divine is God and God alone: a transcendent, personal, and eternal reality. Heaven and earth are created by Him and are governed by His Providence. Here, then, from the very beginning we find the exclusion of a dualism which professes that what is proper and supreme in man is something eternal and divine, and no hint that man must be saved from his earthly captivity.

Man is of the earth. He is "Adam": that is, made by God from the earth and called to life by Him. His life, at the beginning, is viewed and esteemed only from the viewpoint of the earth. "We the living" are those who enjoy the sunshine and the goods of the earth. Salvation is the earthly well-being of this people. It is kept and cherished by God when it remains faithful to his Covenant with Him, but it is threatened as soon as God deserts it on account of its disobedience.

Man is a unity of animated bodily being. In the Old Testament "soul and spirit" do not refer to an immaterial part that constitutes man along wih a corporal part. "Soul" usually means the whole of man in his personal living existence, and "spirit" signifies rather the principle of life as an active power. The fundamental idea seems to be that of "life" and "life-force." Life exists in its maximum intensity in God. From Him and by Him it is communicated in varying degrees to created beings. Human life takes on the limited form of embodied life here on earth. Hence there is a certain distinction between man's life and its expression in the body. Just as life descends to a lower intensity in fatigue and sleep, so in death it reaches a minimum of intensity and has the character of a profound sleep from which only God can awaken it. In that perspective another life in the full sense is unthinkable, except by resurrection.

Nevertheless, human life is something unique in comparison with that of other beings on earth. It is a self-conscious life, a life in which man is able to place himself interiorly at a certain distance from himself. Man can reflect within himself, in his heart, about the way he will act. He can be so foolish as to say in his heart: "There is no God." The heart is the inner sphere in which man makes his good or evil plans. Man, then, is free; he has the power of obediently directing his life according to God's will or rising in disobedience against God. He can lose control over himself and his life so that he comes under the influence of other powers, of evil powers that lead to perdition, or of a good power, the spirit of God, who increases his life and makes him capable of extraordinary deeds.

That is why man occupies a unique place in the world. He is the viceregent, the agent of God upon earth. For he was created "after God's likeness." This idea has something to do with man's erect figure, his frank appearance, his physical beauty and bodily expressiveness. The fundamental point, however, is that man is appointed by God to rule over the earth, over plants and animals, and to use them under the supreme dominion of God, the Lord of all creation. Thus Genesis, Chapter 1:26 and 28, signifies that man was given the genuine task of subduing the earth. "And as the appraisal of God's creation is good, very good, so also civilization is given a positive appraisal. It is the fulfillment of God's command: 'Replenish the earth and subdue it.' "[4] Man's task contains also an admonition to fight against dangerous and powerful forces that exist in the world and in man himself: "If you do well, will you not be accepted; but if you do not well, will not sin crouch at the door! Its desire is for you, but you must master it" (Gen. 4:7). Sin has bad consequences for man which he must overcome by strenuous efforts and struggle.

Man, therefore, received the commission to bring nature and his own being under his dominion by a life of struggle in the world. He is a king in creation. "The Lord from the earth created man. . . . He endows man . . . with power over all things else on earth. In his own image He made him. . . . He puts the fear of him in all flesh, and gives him

---

[4]L. Köhler, *Old Testament Theology,* London, 1957, p. 147.

rule over beasts and birds" (Sirach, 17:1-4). Hence man is Lord of the earth by his intelligent and wise rule, by his struggle and his culture. This lordship defines what his original nature is in virtue of creation; and that which exists in virtue of creation is not undone by any later development, not even by sin.

Yet sin is an essential characteristic of the Old Testament image of man. It consists in man, created by God to rule over the earth in God's name, turning against Him as an independent master in an attitude of disobedience and rebellion. Man wishes to be independent in his domain, he wishes to be like God. Sin leaves its mark on man: the desire to sin, the attachment to sin and finally obduracy in sin. As Jeremia tells us, the heart of Israel is corrupt and hardened in its corruption. In that sense sin belongs to the actual nature of man, is not according to the way God created him, but the way man fashioned himself. That sinfulness infects his whole life and his culture.

Sin is closely connected with salvation. Sin is followed by punishment; God abandons His people to its enemies. But He remains faithful to His Covenant and His promises. He invites His people to return to Him and promises salvation from slavery. This promise becomes an eschatological vision in Deutero-Isaia. A situation is envisaged there in which the people will be freed not only from the bondage that is a result of sin, but will be freed from sin itself. This salvation will not be for Israel alone but for man, that is, for all mankind.

5. FROM A FUNCTIONAL TO A PERSONALISTIC COMMUNITY

Everything we have said applies not merely to man as an individual but also to the community. Man enjoys life within the group and, in the beginning, his character is also judged according to the group: "In the Old Testament it is taken for granted that *man lives in a community,* comprehensive to a degree we can scarcely imagine."[5]

---

[5]Köhler, *op. cit.* p. 161.

In ever widening circles the individual is in a union of life and heart with the community, both in the present (the family, the tribe) and in the past (forefathers). His evil and good deeds are attributed to the group and the group is rewarded or punished for them. Within the Covenant also, man at first does not stand before God as an individual but as a people. Groups are described as persons. The praying "I" of the Psalms often coincides, with the "we" of the community. The whole community is concentrated in the praying king or priest.

Morality too is social. "All moral ideas of the Bible have a strikingly sociological character. A just or right deed is a deed that is in harmony with the life of the group. An evil deed, on the contrary, harms the coherence of the community. That is why it must be condemned."[6]

The sociological problem of the Old Testament is not so much, "How can several individuals form a community together?", but rather, "How can an individual come forward in the community as having a personal value and a personal responsibility?" In regard to this point we notice that there is a gradual development. At the beginning the individual almost merges with the group. For example, Achan, who through his theft had brought down Yahweh's anger upon Israel, is destroyed by fire "with all that is his" and all his kin (Josue 7:10-26). Good also is credited to the group. The truly just one is not punished with the wicked, but the wicked are saved because of the just one. For ten just men Yahweh is willing to save Sodom and Gomorrha. We see here a trend that leads to the recognition of the individual's value. We notice already in the Book of Kings how human individuals stand in the foreground with their personal character, their personal merit or demerit. The house of David is a family of very differentiated personalities. In fact, so much attention is given to the

---

[6]See G. Pidoux, L'homme dans l'Ancien Testament, J. C. Bleeker, ed., *Anthropologie religieuse,* Leiden, 1955, p. 165.

human and the individual that it has been possible to speak of a "Solomonic humanism."

During the Babylonian Captivity, when the calamity that afflicted the community caused a wavering of the faith in Yahweh, it was particularly Ezechiel who stressed the importance of the individual human being: every person is rewarded or punished for his own deeds, not for the actions of others or for those of his ancestors.[7] The individual can restore his good relations with God by personal conversion. Nevertheless, the moral and religious individual still appears within the common framework of the group's salvation history. However, in the Book of Job and in some of the later Psalms, the righteous individual seems to stand totally alone before God in a purely vertical relation with Him, outside of any common framework of the group's salvation history.

The individual man is also singled out from the group because of a special vocation. The prophet is separated from the group in a way that is painful to him and he is placed over against the people as the bearer of God's word. However, this separation is not for his own individual salvation or in view of a mystical union with God, but because of a public mission and in view of the salvation of the community. But prophetism points to a future when all will be personally filled by God. As the book of Jeremia says: "No longer will they have need to teach their friends and kinsmen how to know the Lord. All from least to greatest shall know me, says the Lord, for I will forgive their evil-doing and remember sin no more" (Jeremia, 31:34).

We see therefore that the Old Testament view regarding man's social character underwent a striking development. Slowly man emancipated himself from the anonymity of the primitive group, as an independent responsible person who possessed an inalienable personal value. Reward and punishment, God's grace and man's answer to grace,

---

[7]Cf. e.g., Ch. F. Whitly, *The Exilic Age,* London, 1957, pp. 82-117.

all these became personalized. This development gave a definitive clarification regarding the relation between the individual and the group. This growth did not mean, however, that there was a change in God's Revelation, but only that Israel's life matured under the attractive and inviting influence of God's word.

Unlike the Koran, the Old Testament is not a divine monologue but the inspired account of a dialogue between God and His chosen people. The Bible is not God's written self-revelation. The Bible contains God's word of Revelation but as digested in the maturing life of Israel. The word of God penetrated into the life of His people, adapted itself to the psychological and moral development of the Hebrew, and guided that development in the direction desired by divine Providence.

6. The Humanism of Israel

The world is God's work of creation. That is why it is good. The earth is good. Man is good. The life of man upon earth is good. These statements contain the fundamental conditions of every genuine humanism.

Life presented itself to man first of all as an earthly life. Originally the perspective of human existence was purely earthly; man was God's viceregent on earth. In obedience to God's plan, he had the duty to establish his dominion over the earth and over his own life. God first manifested Himself as Creator and Lord and then later, and fully so in the New Testament, He revealed Himself as the intimate supraearthly end of man's life. Similarly, He first impressed upon man the goodness and meaningfulness of his earthly life and then revealed to him a vocation of life which must be fulfilled within this earthly existence but which, at the same time, also transcends the earth. In this way Israel received the perspective of a humanism that had its roots in religion but that could later be broadened into Christian humanism.

Man sinned. Instead of playing the role of second master under God, he wanted to be the first master of the earth against God. Herein lies the great temptation of humanism. Here is traced the path that later was to lead to a closed, earthly and atheistic humanism. The dispersed children of Israel would play a great role in the earthly development of that closed humanism. By doing so, they too would remain within the perspective of biblical history.

Under the guidance of God's word the consciousness of the Hebrew developed from primitive collectivism to an open personalism in which man stood before God with a fully affirmed and responsible personal dignity. No longer did he live solely as a member of an ethnical group; but he stood apart, called in full freedom to enter into communion with God and form a community with his fellow-men. A communion of persons is the great and ideal value of genuine humanism. In Israel the ideal was only in a state of gestation. In Christ it was to be realized by grace and charity, but in a community which, although incarnate in the earthly forms of life, is no longer of this world but is a "kingdom of heaven." However, in the light of the heavenly kingdom of love, man's earthly project was to be clarified and permeated with the idea of communion of love as the ideal for every genuine community of men.

Although Israel turned away from God by sin, God remained faithful to the Covenant and His promises. He revealed the greatness of His heart ever more fully to the sinful and then again repentant people. Finally Israel became the bearer of the most sublime promises destined for all mankind: salvation, not only from punishment for sin but also from guilt; a communion with God in which man would be taught immediately by God's light and directed to Him by His attraction. The Church of Pentecost would live in the consciousness that those promises were truly realized in her.

In this way the personal community of men is taken up into a direct personal communion with God, and humanism is achieved in something that is more than pure humanism.

7. THE PROBLEM OF THE NEW TESTAMENT

In following the further development of the biblical doctrine concerning the earthly community as it is found in the New Testament, we must first of all recall how insistently Christ Himself declared that He had not come to destroy but to fulfill.

Nevertheless, we must ask ourselves whether God's entrance into historical mankind was not bound to break through and abolish Old Testament humanism from within. Doesn't new wine break old wineskins? For the fulfillment that Christ brought did not spring from the earth but came from above and invaded history. Christ came from God. Where He appeared, heaven came close. By His Incarnation He established the "kingdom of heaven" on earth. Hence the fulfillment He brought was not earthly but supernatural The community in which He gathered us is not a community of earthly people but a community of the people of God whose "home" is not on earth but in heaven. Are we not transferred by Him from the kingdom of earth into an eschatological kingdom that is no longer of the earth? Does the shadow not yield before the light, and the symbol before reality?

Undoubtedly Christ's coming produced a tension between the earthly community with its earthly perspective and the heavenly community with its vision of eternity. Life in the period of the final kingdom as begun but not yet historically completed, the period between the first and the second coming of Christ, is truly paradoxical. However, it can be shown, we think, that the biblical humanism of the Old Testament is not abolished but fulfilled in that paradoxical situation. The union of God and man, of heaven and earth, in Christ, gives to man's earthly task a higher completive meaning and a definitive possibility of success.

8. MAN AND SIN IN THE NEW TESTAMENT

The Old Testament view of man is preserved in the New Testament, but its development is now determined by the Incarnation of the Word who entered history and brought the definitive Revelation of God's plan of salvation.

It is no longer possible to doubt that the doctrine of the New Testament agrees with that of the Old. St. Paul, in whom anthropological ideas were most fully developed, used the anthropological terminology that, most of the time, is in full agreement with the Old Testament, in spite of some Greek nuances: "diverse ways in which man, the 'I,' can be considered, appear in the use of the anthropological terms *soma* (body), *psyche* (soul) and *pneuma* (spirit). Man is not composed of two or three parts; still less are *psyche* and *pneuma,* within the *soma,* particular organs or principles of a higher spiritual life that is supposed to transcend animal life. On the contrary, man is a living unity, and 'I,' that can become an object to itself, that has a relation to itself (*soma*) and that is living in its intentionality, in its tending to something, in its willing and knowing (*psyche, pneuma*).[8]" The term "heart" also is used in the same sense as in the Old Testament, although "mind" (*nous*) appears as a second term and puts more stress on knowing in contrast with "heart" which suggests rather the idea of feeling, striving, and willing. A more properly Pauline term borrowed from Jewish Hellenism is that of "conscience": the reflective knowledge and judgment of one's own intended or accomplished deeds. This idea, however, was already present in the Old Testament concept of "heart." Accordingly, we find in St. Paul only a more developed and more differentiated terminology to express the Israelitic view about man.

Paul's deeper insight into the nature of sin is also only a further development of the Old Testament concept. Sin is essentially pride: man refuses to live his life as a gift of God but lives it as something he wants to possess and administer independently and for himself. It is disobedience, rebellion, the will to independence. However, St. Paul does

---

[8]R. Bultmann, *Theologie des Neuen Testaments,* Tübingen, 1953, pp. 205-206.

not see sin exclusively as a turning away from God by which pagans delivered themselves to idolatry and immorality. Sin is also the pharisaical boasting about one's own virtue, wisdom, justice, good works, pneumatic endowments, which man arrogates to himself as if he had earned them by his own merits. Thus all men, both Jews and pagans, have fallen under the power of sin and need the salvation of Christ.

In the light of the Christian Revelation of salvation, St. Paul sees sinful existence as a "life according to the flesh." The term "flesh" signifies man insofar as he is involved in earthly, temporal, perishable existence. The realm of the flesh is the world, the ensemble of earthly possibilities with all the structures and powers that belong exclusively to the earth. The "flesh" and the "world" are not evil in themselves. Man here below must of necessity "walk in the flesh," that is, be man. But "to live according to the flesh" or according to the world is evil, for it means that man proudly devotes his attention and his thought, his care and concern, exclusively to his own kingdom, to this earthly existence, to earthly goods of life. He thus shuts himself off from the kingdom of God, from Christian salvation, which is to live with the risen Christ in God.

Accordingly, the "flesh" and the "world" are terms of condemnation only to the extent that they signify a life directed purely to what is human and motivated by purely earthly cares and norms. This vision is essential to the formation of a Christian view of culture and social life on earth, for it sharply defines the problem of our relation to earthly and historical reality. This clear formulation is the more necessary because the world is seen as a supra-personal, social force that, not of itself but by man's sin, is in conflict with God. By sin there becomes incarnate in the human community a "spirit of the world," a worldly atmosphere to which every man contributes by his personal sins while, on the other hand, undergoing its baneful influence.

Thus, on the level of earthly existence man is, in a certain sense, delivered to sin. By his situation in the sinful community of which he is a part, he is in some measure estranged from himself. He does not have full power to dispose of his own being, but he lives under foreign powers in which Satan is at work. And Satan sometimes, as in the case of possession, gains complete control over him. This idea of a sinful, demonic world that wars against God and Christ, but from which we are liberated by Christ and with which we may henceforth have no communion, is expressed with special forcefulness in St. John's dualistic formulae.

Hence the great ontological and moral abyss that, according to the New Testament, is found in reality, does not run straight through man but yawns between man and God. However, this abyss is seen exclusively in a historical perspective of salvation: "The whole man, with his body and soul, is called upon to obey God. . . . With his whole person, with his body, but also with his soul, also with his human spirit, he is sinful before God. . . . The whole man, body and soul and spirit, has need of salvation. . . . The only important boundary line, according to the New Testament, is not drawn between various parts of the human being, but between the whole man, body, soul and spirit on the one hand, and, on the other, that which comes from God, that which God bestows through Christ."[9]

9. THE HEAVENLY COMMUNITY AND THE CHURCH

The New Testament gives no direct attention to the human community on the level of the world (*mundus*), of earthly existence. This existence is not looked at nor judged in itself, in its proper nature. Principally it is looked at in its sinful corruption, as a situation of perdition from which man is saved by Christ. Direct attention is given to man's new social being, the heavenly and eschatological community, in which man is taken up by Christ's salvation. For the Christian, Revelation is indeed the revelation of the "kingdom of heaven" that has come into and established itself in the world

---

[9] J. N. Sevenster, "Die Anthropologie des Neuen Testaments," *Anthropologie religieuse,* Leiden, 1955, pp. 169, 171, 172.

with Christ and also in and through Him. This kingdom is not of this world but it really enters this world and becomes incarnate in the historical forms of existence in this world.

From the standpoint of comparative religion the proper character of Christianity can be described more or less in the following terms: "As an incarnational religion Christianity offers as the divine end and purpose, not the absorption of the human into the divine, not the extinction of human personality, nor an eternity of bliss after death as the reward of a virtuous life on earth, but a living union with God here and now, a life already belonging to the timeless realm in which the human spirit, freed from the bondage of sin, enriched by the knowledge of God, will develop to the utmost in communion with all the other spirits moving toward the same goal, to the full potentialities with which grace has endowed it."[10] This description is true if we understand the word "spirit" in the biblical sense.

The heavenly community as it appears in its earthly form has an ontological foundation, viz., the new creation by which we, in the core of our manhood, are made one and alike in a new spiritual race, the race of Christ, a race in which all the differences, inequalities and divisions according to the flesh, that is, according to this temporal earthly existence, are removed and made irrelevant.

From this ontological foundation of grace springs man's new social existence, namely, to be the people of God, the Church. The Church is a visible society. It spreads through preaching over the whole world and is hierarchically and socially organized like a body that has many members and functions. We become members through faith and baptism. We are nourished in it by the Holy Eucharist: the sacramental communion with God through the risen Lord, Jesus Christ. He made His sacrificed body and blood be our food, that is, the source of a power of life in the order of the new existence He has given us.

---

[10] S. H. Hooke, *The Siege Perilous. Essays in Biblical Anthropology,* London, 1956, pp. 259-260.

The bond of that perfect community is charity, the theological virtue of love. This love is the proper exercise of the new way of existence acquired by grace and of the power of life given us in the Eucharist. The Christian must be clothed with Christ, as St. Paul tells us, that is, he must exercise all human virtues but after the manner of Christ. This manner is the way of love. The proper characteristic of the phenomenon of Christian life is love. It is only through a love that inspires and embraces everything that man's character is Christian.

We see here how the New Testament continues and perfects the Old Testament. We saw how in the Old Testament the individual left behind the anonymity of the group and acquired a dignity of his own. At the end, the just man stood almost hopelessly alone before God in a corrupted world. The religious community was only a promise, a beautiful promise, an eschatological reality; all were to be called once, in order to be freed from sin, and to be instructed immediately by God Himself. The Church of Pentecost lives in the consciousness that that prophecy is fulfilled in her. Peter's first sermon precisely applies the prophecy of Joel to the happenings of Pentecost: "I will pour forth of my Spirit upon all flesh. . . . And moreover upon my servants and upon my handmaids in those days will I pour forth of my Spirit and they shall prophesy" (Acts 2: 17-18). In St. John's gospel we hear Christ alluding to the prophecy of Isaia (Is. 54:11-15) according to which all who build the new Sion of precious stones will be personally taught by God. "It is written in the prophets, 'And they shall all be taught of God.' Everyone who has listened to the Father, and has learned, comes to me" (Jo. 6:45). Under the influence of preaching comes faith, not as a social opinion, but as a personal conviction that is formed in man by the inner attraction and enlightenment of the Father.[11] And in his first letter St. John

[11]Concerning the relation between preaching and the light of faith, between external relevation and inner enlightenment, cf. the author's forthcoming article on the development of doctrine in *The New Catholic Encyclopedia* under *Doctrine*.

adds that we have received an unction of the Holy Spirit, who instructs us interiorly, and that therefore it is not necessary that anyone should teach us (1 Jo. 2:20-21, 27). In this way is accomplished the transition from the functionalistic community, in which the individual was merely a function of the group, to a personalistic community, in which man, as an independent person established in the freedom and certainty of faith by God Himself, can form a community of love with his brethren.

10. CHRISTIAN SALVATION AND EARTHLY VALUES

It follows that the personalistic community of salvation, realized in time, is the proper content of Christian Revelation. But it is impossible that Revelation should not indirectly shed some light on the earthly existence of man and on the historical tasks and social structures that belong to this existence. If the life of the Christian is raised to a higher, super-historical level, the problem concerning his attitude to historical life becomes the more pressing. For here on earth he continues to "walk in the flesh." Although he is member of the Church, he remains also a member of a family, a people, a state, a community of culture. Moreover, the Church herself is realized "in the flesh," in earthly forms of this world. It is therefore to be expected that the fundamental relationship of the Christian and the Church to the tasks and to the forms of life that belong to historical existence will be illuminated to some extent by Christ's Revelation.

First of all, what judgment is made on the basis of faith about earthly life, abstracting from and, as it were, preceding the event of Christian salvation? As we have seen, the whole world was thought of as being in the bondage of sin. This judgment, however, in no way detracts from the judgment which the Creator pronounced about His works: "God saw that all He had made was very good" (Gen. 1:31). The world and man, as God created them, were good and remain good.

Sin is the cause of evil, but sin does not affect the inherent goodness created in man and in the world. No doubt, sin has given rise to certain structures in the world that do not correspond to the original will of the Creator. This statement applies even to some Jewish institutions which God permitted on account of the "wickedness of the human heart," and which in reality are compromises lying midway between God's original will, aiming at the ideal, and the concrete possibilities of a weak and unwilling heart. Christ made a distinction between God's original institutions and the concessions of Moses or the traditions of the teachers. To the carnal law with its external observances, St. Paul opposed God's spiritual agreement with Abraham: "Thus a deeper layer appears under the institutions of Judaism. The work of God was partly falsified by institutions. . . . Man is better than what the institutions have made of him."[12] St. Paul likewise expresses his great esteem for the Greek and Roman cultural values, in spite of his passionate rejection of idolatry. "He senses the culture of 'humanity' above and beyond paganism."[13]

If this is so, then the original work of creation, which remains underneath the stained cover of sinful existence, longs for the glory of the sons of God (Rom. 8:21-23). And this includes all creation, not merely irrational nature, but man also in all the natural dimensions of his earthly existence. If salvation from sin and the attitude of love can become a reality in men who here below walk in the flesh, it follows that this Christian "walking in the flesh" will inevitably affect and transform the world which is the domain of the flesh. "Hence precisely the earthly relations must share in the freedom that was given to faith (1 Cor. 7:29-51). Just as the apostle is related to the congregation, so is the Christian individual related to the world—in the sense that the Christian guards and preserves the character of God's creation in the

---

[12]L. Cerfaux, "La situation du chrétien dans le monde d'après le Nouveau Testament," *Tolerance et communauté humaine* (Cahiers de l'actualité religieuse), Tournai, pp. 51-52.
[13]*Ibidem,* p. 51.

world, whereas the apostle wishes to see that the congregations are the people of God or the property of Christ."[14]

This quotation expresses the matter very well. There is no question here of a work of the Church for which the ecclesiastical authorities are responsible; but it concerns a task which the Christian individual, especially the layman, enjoying the freedom of the children of God and under the guidance of his conscience, must accomplish according to concrete circumstances. The liberation of the biblical world (*mundus*) is therefore a self-evident, though ever imperfect, overflow or repercussion of a salvation which the Church possesses perfectly, in the earthly community of which those who are saved form a part: "The victory of Christ is complete in the Church; she is freed from the devil and from evil powers. And because this spiritual sphere, spiritually liberated, completely permeates the temporal, a relative liberation of the temporal is accomplished by it."[15]

The liberation of culture, the restoration of its original movement toward the good, is a real tendency of the kingdom of God in its earthly incarnation. But concretely speaking, that liberation is far from complete. Although the devil is already overcome and doomed to perdition, he still has some liberty and power in the world. The "mystery of iniquity" will remain active until Christ's final return, and it will continue to win many apparent victories. Hence the Christians, who as members of the earthly Church live under the influence of a world that is only partly saved, are not free from the spirit of sin. Thus the world to some extent veils the unstained and unwrinkled countenance of Christ's Bride on earth.

For this reason the Church assumes a twofold attitude toward the world and its powers. She tries to protect her members, according to the circumstances and the demands

---

[14]E. Fuchs, "Gemeinschaft und Individuum im A.T.," in Kurt Galling, *Die Religion in Geschichte und Gegenwart*, vol. II, 3rd ed., Tübingen, 1958, col. 1356.

[15]Cerfaux, *op. cit.*, p. 54.

of the historical situation, against the bad influence of the world; but, on the other hand, she also encourages them to exercise a good influence upon this world.

11. CHURCH AND STATE

The Church's attitude toward earthly powers is likewise twofold and somewhat variable. The New Testament accepts the state as an earthly institution that exists in virtue of the order of creation. Hence the state has an unconditional power over individuals in the earthly, temporal sphere; it serves their interests by limiting their arbitrariness and by guiding life in an orderly way. But the state is not the ultimate reality by which man lives nor the highest authority to which he must be obedient. Above life in the temporal world, which is subject to the power of the state, there is a life based on the eternal Truth, that directly obeys the God from whom the state itself has received its existence and its power.

Moreover, since the Resurrection, the power of the state is subject to *Kyrios,* the Lord Jesus Christ. To Him all power in heaven and on earth has been given (Mat. 28:15). All created power must bend the knee before Him and acknowledge Him as Lord (Phil. 2:10). Everything in heaven and on earth is reconciled in Him with God (Col. 1:14). The royal dominion of Christ extends beyond the domain of the Church. Not only Church authority but secular authority is exercised in Christ's name. Any good exercise of authority is a service of the Lord.

On the other hand, however, it is especially in the sins of the state that the sin of the world shows its diabolical countenance. That sin consists in the fact that the state, which has received power from God over earthly matters, withdraws from all submission, bases its power on itself, and wishes even to bring the regulation of man's relation with God under its own control. It thus imposes itself on mankind as an all-embracing institution of salvation and makes itself the center of all religious bonds. As a consequence the state is led to condemn Christ and persecute the Church, whose very nature is a condemnation of the state's totalitarian ambition. In this way the state comes to appear as the antichrist.[16]

It was in such a situation that Christianity arose and developed. Its solemn profession *"Kyrios Christus"* (Christ is the Lord) must be seen in contrast with the cry *"Kyrios Kaisar"* and *"Kaisar theos"* (Caesar is the Lord, Caesar is God).[17] By claiming absolute and totalitarian power, the state makes itself an earthly god and tries to keep man's life imprisoned in an earthly existence. The state thus becomes the social incarnation of the "spirit of the world" that is delivered to demonic powers. It then represents the "kingdom of Satan" as the absolute adversary of the "kingdom of God."

Accordingly, the relation of the Church and the Christian to the state is manifold. The general relation is expressed with sufficient clearness in the words of Our Lord: "Render therefore to Caesar the things that are Caesar's, and to God the things that are God's" (Mk. 12:17). Man is obliged to give obedience and respect to the state and its representatives in the order of earthly life that is directed to historical purposes and the earthly well-being of the human community. That attitude is not inspired by indifference, for the power of the state represents the order of the Creator and the kingship of Christ. For this reason we must submit to the lawful exercise of state authority with loving submission to God and Christ. But in the order of salvation, of the eternal communion with God in Christ, we must obey God and His Church. When the state goes counter to that, we must obey God rather than men, and must be willing to accept martyrdom, that is, to give a crowning testimony of our life proclaiming that Christ is the Lord.

---

[16]Cf. H. Schlier, "Vom Antichrist," *Die Zeit der Kirche,* Freiburg, 1956, pp. 16-29.

[17]Cf. O. Cullmann, *Die Christologie des Neuen Testaments,* 2nd ed., Tübingen, 1958, pp. 234-235.

The Church's attitude toward the state is likewise twofold. When and to the extent that the state as an anti-Christian power opposes her or her task, the Church must condemn the state in God's name and, in that respect, refuse and forbid cooperation with the state. This attitude of condemnation is most clearly and most radically expressed in the Apocalypse. However, the Church will cooperate with the state to the extent that the latter exercises a legitimate authority. For the state's aim is to promote the true good of man's life. Life is one. The Christian's life is not cut off from earthly goods and human values, but includes them. Christ the King is not divided against Himself in the distinction between Church and state. The ideal remains mutual cooperation, in obedience to the same Lord and in unity of service to the same total well-being of man.[18]

12. CHRISTIAN FREEDOM IN THE TEMPORAL ORDER

We find, then, a clear norm in the New Testament for the general relationship between Christianity and the values and powers of earthly existence. But we would look in vain for a theoretical and practical doctrine concerning the inner ordering of earthly life itself. This inner order lies outside the perspective of Revelation, which deals exclusively with matters of direct concern to Christian salvation and the social existence of man in the kingdom of God. The theory and practice of the earthly order of life is left to the efforts of man's own existence, which thinks and develops in constant historical growth, and to the prudence and conscience of free responsible persons.

It is remarkable how St. Paul gives no particular prescriptions in God's or Christ's name regarding earthly life in the human community. He merely asks us to follow the virtuous norms that are generally accepted also by sincere pagans: "For the rest, brethren, whatever things are true, whatever honorable, whatever just, whatever holy, whatever

---

[18]Cf. H. Schlier, "Die Beurteilung des Staates im Neuen Testament," *Die Zeit der Kirche,* pp. 1-16.

lovable, whatever of good repute, if there be any virtue, if anything worthy of praise, think upon these things" (Phil. 4:8). Christian righteousness within the order of earthly social life is not fundamentally different from the civil righteousness of the pagan. The only profound difference lies in the all-embracing meaning and direction that love gives to the total character of man. Love sums up in itself all virtues and gives them a higher motive; it also gives them a supernatural meaning and value. It gives to the Christian life a characteristic mark by which it is sharply distinguished from the pagan style of life, even in the latter's most noble expressions.

Hence we must not be astonished when we do not find in the New Testament revolutionary declarations or propaganda regarding the things that belong to the earthly order of existence. Even the slavery that forms a part of the established order is neither disapproved nor abolished. It is only said that those who within the earthly sphere are in the positions of lord or servant, stand together before the Lord as equals and brothers in the order of salvation and the community of Christ. The only practical lines of conduct for earthly life found in the New Testament are those adapted to the situation that existed at that time. Occasionally Christians are told how they can best live as Christians within the established order.

It would be wrong, therefore, to make a collection of the practical counsels given in the New Testament for the conduct of Christians in the world and, then, look upon them as a specific Christian doctrine having universal validity. It would be unreasonable to conceive and absolutize the concrete established relations between master and slave, man and woman, lord and subject, that form the background of New Testament admonitions, as if they pertained to the Christian deposit of Revelation. All those regulations and relations have a historical and variable character and are subject to the law of historical development. In the environment of the New Testament, the small Christian minority was not yet in a situation in which a creative organizing and fashioning of earthly life could pose a practical problem for Christians.

The time for such an intervention develops eventually and Christians would then be faced with the task of freeing the original order of creation from all sorts of institutional distortions. They will then have to accept the charge given by God in *Genesis* to man as his representative on earth, they will then have to create a culture according to the pure intention of the Creator and in the spirit of Christian love and obedience. This the Christians will have to do on their own responsibility, according to ever clearer insights gained progressively by thinking man. They will have to do this by using the methods and techniques required by the nature and laws that are proper to each field of endeavor.

This autonomous, socio-ethical and socio-technical thought will follow the general guidance of the Christian ethics of love and faith in our Christian vocation, both of which contain an implicit confirmation of the inviolable value of the human person. The analogy between the order of grace and the order of creation will help the theologian to explain the content of Revelation with the help of the categories of historical thinking. But it will also prompt the Christian philosopher and sociologist to acquire a more correct understanding of the nature of man, the foundations of the social order, and the objectives of culture.

13. SUMMARY

We have asked ourselves what value judgment Holy Scripture expresses regarding the earthly existence of man and what meaning it attaches to that existence. The answer was as follows:

1. Man's earthly existence is good in itself because God gave him this existence in creation. This implies that his existence in the natural connections of the earthly community are likewise good. For man's earthly existence is by its very nature a social life.

2. The meaning attributed to earthly existence is that
of man's royal dominion over the earth. This dominion
man must excercise as the agent of God, hence with submission to the divine will as expressed in the order of creation and with active recognition of God's glory. That
dominion has been entrusted to man as a task, as a command. This task he must realize with his intelligence and
free will according to a moral code. Thus this task is culture. It is also a form of freedom, for to rule over the world
means to have the management of one's own life insofar as
it is a life in the world.

3. Man's sin is a proud disobedience by which he wishes
to have dominion over the world and, hence, free control over
his own life in his own name and for himself, independently of God and even against Him. That sin characterizes
and colors man's life in this world, determines the situation
of the earthly community and the development of its institutions. Human life becomes a sinful existence, a life according to the flesh in a sinful world.

4. The Revelation of man's religious salvation, by which
man is taken up into a spiritual and eschatological community,
the kingdom of God, does not mean a cancellation of the
order of creation. The original task of earthly existence is
not withdrawn but proclaimed in a new way: as a relative salvation of the earthly community and as a restoration
of the first purpose of creation.

5. The revelation of the Christian vocation, which is
a work of grace, emphasizes at the same time the inviolable
dignity of the human person. We saw how the individual,
as revealed in Scripture, appears with increasing personal
responsibility and value. The dignity of the person is definitively established by the revelation of the dignity man has
in the eyes of God. Thus it is clear also that this personal
dignity may not be attacked by any earthly power, not
even by that of the state.

6. The Christian vocation that discloses the dignity of the person is a vocation to community. That community to which the person is called is a community of "charity," that is, of the love of friendship with God and with one's fellow-men. In Christ we form one body of love. This love, poured into our hearts by the Holy Spirit, is also the power that liberates man from the sinful individualism of pride. Love thus cures culture or man's development of social existence in its very roots and makes possible once more the original task given to him by creation. This love is an all-embracing disposition that determines our moral attitude as a whole. Therein lies the validity of the following analogy: just as love is the bond of the perfect community in the kingdom of God, so is the earthly community directed to the highest moral ideal of a love that can build a genuine community. The revelation of the kingdom of God reveals at the same time that the most profound meaning of the earthly community is to strive to become a kingdom of love.

CHAPTER FIVE

PERSONALISM: METAPHYSICS AND THE GENERAL ETHICS OF THE PERSON

1. TOWARD A CHRISTIAN PHILOSOPHY OF THE SOCIAL ORDER

The purpose of the preceding examination of Scripture was to prepare a modern Christian view of the earthly, temporal community. Before attempting a synthesis, it is necessary clearly to define its scientific status.

As we have seen in Chapter One, the Catholic view concerning the nature of our social life in the earthly sphere is not simply a view of faith. Revelation is concerned with salvation and the community of those who share in it. The essence of our natural social life and the norms that must regulate our temporal community in this world are not the proper object of Christian Revelation. Hence the Catholic view we have in mind here is also the result of man's own thinking, the result of autonomous human thought, but in the light of what God has revealed concerning man and his vocation.

No doubt, there is a dialectical relationship between that autonomous thought of the Christian and the Revelation of God. However, this relationship, like any other truly dialectical relationship, does not affect the proper nature and autonomy of the two thoughts engaged in the dialogue. Thus the thinking from which the Catholic view of the earthly human community is born remains an autonomous human reflection.

It follows that the Catholic view is not theological but is and remains philosophical. Theology by reflection clarifies the data of faith; philosophy sheds light on natural experience. But, because of the dialectical relationship between the philosophical and the theological thinking of the Christian, such a philosophy can rightly be called Christian or Catholic. For it is part of a single total movement of thought springing from a single Christian personality.

At this point, we have no desire to discuss at length the debated problem of "Christian philosophy." Consequently, we shall confine ourselves to a few remarks indicating what we mean by that term. The author agrees with Father D. de Petter that the authentic philosophizing of a Christian believer is necessarily a Christian philosophizing. This statement expresses what all Christian philosophers actually do and is therefore a declaration of common sense. If a believer tries to "bracket" his faith when he philosophizes, he either destroys his personal attitude of belief or his philosophizing is not authentic, that is, he deprives his thought of a truly philosophical character. For, as we saw in Chapter One, philosophical thought arises from a questioning within the concrete historical situation and the personal experience of the philosophizing man. Now, for a believing Christian, being-a-believer is "one of the essential aspects of the situation in which his philosophizing takes place and of the personal experience from which an authentic philosophizing cannot be separated."[1]

This does not mean that the Christian philosopher must borrow from his faith theses which he cannot justify on the basis of philosophy. This would be against the nature of philosophy. Nor does it follow that he must try to reduce the mysteries of faith to philosophical insights. This would conflict with the nature and demands of faith. But while philosophizing according to the strict rules of insight, he will attune his thinking to his faith, not only by not affirming anything that is in conflict with it, but also by remaining open to every insight that is in accord with the faith and receptive to every enrichment of his experience and thought under the indirect light of Revelation. At the same time he will scrupulously avoid giving philosophical support to anything which seems to favor his faith when such support is not reasonably justifiable. It is preferable to tolerate the tensions that might arise between our faith and our philo-

---

[1] D. de Petter, "Het philosopheren van de gelovige," in *Tijdschrift voor Philosophie,* vol. XXI (1959), pp. 3-19.

sophical thinking than to deny that tension or attempt to eliminate it by erroneous arguments.

Let it be understood, then, that the synthesis we are about to give is a Christian and Catholic view but not an ecclesiastical one nor a "social doctrine of the Church." The latter expression is always somewhat ambiguous although, if properly understood, it can be used to indicate a definite synthesis of ideas—namely, those found in the documents of the ecclesiastical hierarchy and particularly in the pronouncements of the popes and councils.

However, two ambiguities must be avoided in the use of this term. First, we must avoid giving the impression that here we have a social doctrine being imposed upon us through obedience to faith by the infallible authority of the Church. No doubt there exist certain points which are proposed infallibly by the teaching authority of the Church; but those points do not constitute a doctrine. A Christian doctrine is the fruit of Christian reflection, in the light of faith, upon our earthly experience, as that reflection has developed historically until this day.

This idea points to a second ambiguity that must also be avoided. The Church, in the true sense of that word, is not the Church government or Church authority, but it is the Christian people, the "people of God," that is, the whole body of the faithful. Hence, the term "ecclesial" applies not only to the thought of the hierarchy but to the whole of thought of the believing Church: the thought of her theologians, philosophers and sociologists in the measure in which, under the guidance of faith and in subjection to Church authority, they try to explain their actual experience by authentic reflection in order to outline and solve the great practical problems and tasks of the moment. The Church government speaks on the basis of that thought and in union with the whole body of those who think "in the faith" when it proposes to the faithful some fundamental propositions and theses of social philosophy and gives practical directions. The fact that a pope, drawing from the social thinking of the Catholic communion, formulates certain theses does not, by that very fact, suffice to make these formulas become an immutable norm analogous to pronouncements about the faith.

If the Church authority makes use in her documents of a particular social doctrine, that does not mean that this doctrine now loses its historical character, ceases to be subject to development and variation, and is raised above all critique. This is a very important point, for a mistaken attitude toward doctrines found in the documents of the hierarchy could make us fall into a kind of conservatism, prevent us from keeping up with the rapid progress of the times and playing a leading role in them. The history of the last centuries shows only too clearly that no authority of any kind is able to keep alive what history, that is, "real life," has passed by and transcended.

Two Christian truths of faith will be particularly kept in mind by the Christian philosopher endeavoring to develop a social philosophy in a Christian spirit. The first is the inviolable value of the human person. Since man is created by God and called to live in eternal communion with God Himself, every individual man has in himself a value that surpasses the order of temporal existence and that may not be violated by the social structures of the temporal community. In the light of the destiny for which man is created, the Christian philosopher will penetrate with greater ease into the essence of the person.

The second truth is that man is called to form a "body of love" together with other persons. In the light of this revealed analogy, the Christian philosopher, reflecting on the nature of being-a-person, will dare to affirm that the community of love is simply the perfect state in which the person finally realizes his task of being a person. This does not mean that the person can fully realize in the earthly temporal community that highest, satisfying community for which he by nature longs, and still less that historical mankind, as it actually is, has the capacity to attain this goal.

The Christian philosopher, in cooperation with the theologian, will be prepared to reflect upon the relation between the temporal natural community and the eternal community of grace, in the light of the principles we have developed in Chapter Three, viz., that grace perfects and elevates nature. The natural community of persons calls for a supernatural completion in the saving community of grace and love. That which man, in his total cultural striving directed to a community of persons, ultimately wants and desires, can be satisfactorily realized only through grace, and consequently never by culture alone. This agrees with what de Petter says: "In our opinion, it is right to say that a purely philosophical disclosure of the meaning of human existence shows ultimately a being who is nothing but a fiasco, a being who is unable to realize his most fundamental and essential project by his own powers."[2] This, the last sense in which our philosophical undertaking must be called Christian and Catholic was the aspect stressed and developed by the great Catholic philosopher Maurice Blondel.

2. THE ESSENCE OF THE PERSON

At the beginning of Chapter Two we distinguished four phases in the study of man's social being. We now turn to the first: the development of a personalistic ethics of the community, on the basis of what is proper to man's essence, namely, that he is a person.

The term "person," as has been recognized from ancient times, indicates man's own mode of being. St. Thomas already explained and justified it with perfect clarity. He called the concretely existing being "substance," in the first and proper meaning of the term, or "hypostasis." In describing its nature he always brings out three aspects: "the individual substance, taken up in the definition of the person, implies a *complete* substance, that *subsists* by itself, and is *distinguished* from others."[3]

---

[2]*Ibid.,* p. 17.
[3]*Summa Theologica,* p. III, q. 16, art. 12, *ad* 2.

The substance "subsists," that is, exists in itself. It is that to which existence belongs in the first and true sense. My temperament and my knowledge also exist. But they do not exist in themselves. They exist only as something *of* myself. Their existence must be understood in such a way that something—namely, a substance—exists according to their manner of being. For instance, that man there is lively or slow, cultured or uncultured. Such qualifications do not express something that exists in itself as such, but something that can exist or can be thought only as a way of being of something that exists in itself. "I," on the other hand, do not exist as a way of being *of* something, but I simply exist. A substance, for instance an individual man, exists as "of" itself. This means precisely that the substance does not exist as "*of* something" but *in* itself. The substance is that to which "to be" belongs first and in the proper sense.

That which thus exists in itself is a complete whole. "I" exist in myself with all that can be said about myself, my figure, my temperament, my culture, and with all the parts that constitute my body and my individual nature. "Complete being" here signifies precisely the mode of being proper to the whole in contrast with the mode of being of the part. A corporal part can be severed from the whole of the body and exist apart. A physician can remove an eye and place it on the table. It then exists in itself but no longer as an eye. As an eye, as a part of the body, it exists only in function of the whole, that is, of the organism that sees by means of it. Hence a corporal part is, as such, not a substance, since it exists as belonging to the whole. The substance is a whole that exists in itself.

When I look at that whole in its relation with its environment, there appears at once the third aspect of the substance: the whole exists *apart* or distinct from others. This, of course, must be understood here in a purely ontological way. A substance does not exist as taken up in another substantial whole, but it is not excluded that it can be taken up into a wider and higher relational whole, as when the individual is a part of a community. This third aspect is only an explicitation of something implicitly contained in the first two phases of the description of the substance. The aspect is made explicit in view of Christ, in whom the complete humanity, with all its parts and perfections, exists only as a part *sui generis* of the hypostatic whole of his theandric personality.

Hence "person" means the "individual substance" on the level of free, rational existence. Being a person is a special way of being a substance. This must be understood in the sense that the "existing in itself" that characterizes substance is realized in a most proper way in the person. Here "existing in itself" acquires a strong meaning, a full and strict meaning: "existing in itself" appears in the person as an "acting by and through itself." The person is not a substance in the way of something that exists in itself but in the manner of someone who acts through himself: "In a more special and perfect way the particular and the individual are found in rational substances, which have dominion over their action, and which are not only made to act, as are others, but act of themselves."[4]

The difference is very profound—so deep in fact that there is a most radical line of separation between man and the world below him. The difference affects the first and fundamental way of being, namely, substantiality itself. To act or to do things is the proper "reality" of being. To be is to do something. "To act" is the same as "to be," it is the proper exercise of being. The radical difference between acting through oneself and not acting through oneself but being moved by others, consequently manifests a difference in the first constitutive way of being, in substantiality. Substantiality, being in oneself in the true sense, is acting independently, by and through oneself. Hence substantiality belongs in the true sense to the person alone. The life of an

---

[4]*Summa Theologica*, p. I, q. 29, art. 1. It is difficult to translate the original text: "et non solum aguntur, sicut alia, sed per se agunt."

animal is so much a function of its environment that it is woven into the universal laws of the cosmos, as we have explained in Chapter One. This is why its life is only a part-function of universal life and of the laws that govern the whole of nature. It is not "substantial" in the proper sense of the term. Thus the animal way of being, as manifested in animal life, is not "subsistent."

Hence "substance" is an analogous term; and the person is the first analogate, the one of which that term is predicated in the first place and properly. We apply the term "substance" to lower beings because of some resemblance, but in the animal the proper meaning of the word is not realized. The so-called substantiality of lower beings merely foreshadows substantial existence. It gradually approaches true substantiality in the ascending scale of living beings, without attaining it.

This central ontological insight into the nature of a person must now be developed more fully, especially in respect to the dynamic aspect of acting-through-oneself. It is in this perspective that the ethical reality of being a person will come to light. We will do this in connection with modern personalism and will therefore begin by adopting a more varied terminology in which the terms "individual," "person" and "personality" will acquire distinct shades of meaning.

3. INDIVIDUAL, PERSON, PERSONALITY

"Person" and "personality" are old terms, but in our time they evoke most modern problems. "The rights of the human person," "education for personality" and similar expressions belong to the slogans of our age. One of the most modern movements in the realm of thought is called "personalism." It is a widespread movement with ramifications throughout the world. The Catholic vision likewise adorns itself preferably with the crowning title of personalism.

Whence that actuality? Modern humanity goes forward in the light of two discoveries. It has, first of all, discovered nature with its wonderful laws and possibilities. By a series of revolutions in natural science, our image of the universe has been totally renewed. But the discovery of nature was followed by man's rediscovery of himself. Modern man tries to extricate himself from a materialistic view of the world which reduced him to a mere fragment of material nature. Man finds himself in nature, he is rooted in nature by his bodily being and directed to nature with his whole activity. But he finds himself in nature in his own way. He is not merely a part of it but is in it as a creative freedom which transforms both nature around him and his own nature by means of culture. In this way he makes himself and makes his own world, not through spontaneous evolution but by intelligent, self-responsible effort. This proper characteristic of man's appearance in nature is designated by the word "person." Man is a person, he is called to make himself in this world into a personality, on his own responsibility. Let us explain those terms a little.

"Person" and "personality" signify in different ways the same human whole. Man is, as we have said above, a living whole who exists in himself. But a dog is also such a whole. Both the puppy and the child come into this world as distinct wholes. To be born is to come to exist apart. Man and dog both are therefore distinct wholes in virtue of their birth, of their nature (nature comes from *nasci,* to be born). As such, both form originally natural wholes. Let us designate such a biological natural whole by the word "individual," as in fact is often done in modern personalism.

Both dog and man are individual wholes. But the dog is merely an individual; he is a natural whole and nothing more. At his birth and in virtue of his birth, he is "finished." He has received his whole "capital of life" at birth. Nothing now remains but to unfold that life. What he will be is determined by what he has inherited. No one asks himself anxiously: "What will become of Snoopy?" We know the answer. Snoopy will be like every dog of his breed.

Man, however, is more than an individual, more than that kind of natural whole. In him awakens a self-conscious, thinking freedom. Nothing of what is human is determined in him by birth. He himself must build up his human "capital of life," using efforts and intelligent planning, in the form of self-acquired abilities, knowledge, virtues and attitudes. Whatever he has received from nature, his senses, passions, changing moods, temperament, faculties, the quality of his nerves, become instruments which he must use in the best way through reflective and attentive work. True, the result of his efforts will depend also on the quality of what nature has given him. If he has short legs he has no chance to become a runner; if he has little "gray matter" he will not become a scientific genius; if he has weak nerves he will not become a good pilot. Yet man is for himself a task, a project, a potentiality he must realize by rational effort. To be man means to be called to become more and more man. Now, through that openness, that vocation, based on his intelligence and his freedom, he is more than a natural whole which spontaneously unfolds, he is more than an *individual*. He is a person. Every man is a person. The person is the whole of man, considered as a vocation to rational freedom.

Not every man, however, is a "personality." When I say about someone: "He is quite a personality," I mean, here is one in whom humanity has attained a high degree of realization. Personality thus means a successful achievement of the task given to a person as person. The terms "individual," "person," and "personality" therefore designate always the same human whole: either as the original natural whole (individual), and in that respect man does not differ from the animal; or as a possible higher whole that is a task and a vocation for himself (person), and this is proper to man; or as a realized human completeness (personality), and this is an acquisition of cultivated individuals. Hence, the three terms refer to the same living whole considered on three different levels, viz., the original datum, the task, the realization.

Now in what consists that task and commission which is given to the person and is achieved in personality? As we have said already, it is unification, a making-whole on a higher level. We spontaneously understand by a "personality" a man who is "all of one piece." He knows what he thinks, he has strong convictions. He knows what he wills and is true to himself. All the power he has is used to execute his plan of life. He does not lean this way today and that way tomorrow, but makes a powerful, clear, unambiguous impression on us. He is not lost and mentally submerged in the multitude, nor does he change with the tides of a superficial public opinion. He is truly independent, he is "somebody," he acts from and through himself, he is self-possessed in all his faculties and powers.

He is a man who has himself in hand and remains himself, faithful to his convictions, his ideal, his project of life, whatever may be the changes in his own moods, the emotions of his heart, the outbursts of his nature, whatever may be the reactions of others, the vagaries of public opinion, the changes in circumstances. He stands somewhat above all that: above the vacillating play of the natural forces within himself— these he has in hand, he understands them, dominates them, uses them, knows how to guide them—he stands also above the unsteady play of the world. He is independent, free, firm in his own power. He is and remains himself.

A British thinker has described personality in the following terms: "A mind will be more fully personal the more completely its contemporary states are united with each other to form a single total state, and the more completely its successive total states are united with each other to form the history of a single mind."[5] Hence what characterizes personality is unity in the *now* and unity in *time*. In the personality all powers at each moment are well-ordered. A personality disposes of them as of a disciplined army. Primitive man is what his passionate situation of any particular moment happens to be. If he is furious, he is totally furious and loses himself so totally in his anger that he does things

---

[5]C. D. Broad, *Religion, Philosophy and Physical Research*, London, 1953, p. 161.

for which he retains scarcely any responsibility. He is at every moment what his momentary passion makes him. He does not constitute a whole that possesses itself in an orderly manner, but is now this and then that. Each time he is another being. Today he smiles at you. Tomorrow he may come and murder you. He is unpredictable and unreliable.

On the contrary, the perfect personality is always himself, and totally himself. He has brought all the forces of his being from unconscious darkness into the light of self-knowledge and from wild diffusion to the discipline of a will guided by reason. As a free master he disposes of all the power that constitutes his manhood. His judgment is not falsified or obscured by the cravings and suggestions of momentary passion or emotion, and the application of his powers is not hindered or weakened by outbursts from within nor by obstacles from without. In this consists true freedom: it is not a freedom that is merely openness and possibility, but a freedom that is realization and fulfillment; it is power, ability to dispose of oneself, mastery over one's own deeds, as St. Thomas says, it is a life of self-possession. Such a man can be trusted, one can rely upon him. The animal is predictable because it is without freedom. It has the single-mindedness of nature. The personality too is predictable, but because he is completely free and responsible. He has the single-mindedness of perfect virtue.

4. THE FUNDAMENTAL CHARACTERISTICS OF PERSONALITY

We have seen that being a person means a commission and a task, the successful fulfillment of which is designated by the term "personality." This insight shows at once that the three aspects which St. Thomas distinguishes as the primordial phenomenon of substantiality are realized in a unique fashion in the mode of existence proper to a personal being. As we have explained above, substantiality is properly realized only in the person. The person is substantial as exercising activity through and by himself, that is, in the way of freedom. This freedom, this self-possession of conscious life, is not something that is given but is acquired by the personality. The same must therefore be said of the other aspects of substantiality that are connected with that freedom. For a person, being-complete, wholeness, is not something given, but it is a commission that has to be fulfilled. Man comes into the world as a natural whole in which all the organs and functions are integrated within the one organic life and are directed to the biological good of the individual and the species. The natural perfection of "wholeness" we call bodily health. But man as man becomes aware of the task given him to make of himself a human whole in which the many passions and inclinations of nature are bound together and ordered harmoniously under the rule of a freedom that is guided by reason. This inner unity and concentration of all the vital forms under the power of freedom is acquired only by a slowly-gained insight into the meaning of the spontaneous vital forces and by a facility, won through exercise, in securing the victory of the viewpoint of reason over the deviating viewpoints that are suggested by momentary passions or dispositions of mind.

The harmonious integration of our passions and vital forces in a rational project of life we describe according to its various aspects as so many "virtues." The individual constellation of virtues and vices we gather in the concept of "character." The ideal is the personality, the completely integrated character, the harmoniously ordered unity, the maximal use of our "capital of life" under the rule of freedom. To designate the proper unity of the new wholeness, we also use words and expressions such as "mental balance," "harmony" and "equilibrium."

Finally, the characteristic of existing separately, which St. Thomas gives as the third aspect of substantiality, is found in the personality in a most proper and unique way. The separate existence of the biological individual is based on the principle of individuality: a certain fragment of cosmic matter is taken up into an organism and biologically organized. By this it exists apart from other individuals. In personality, however, "separate existence" means the independence of freedom: the imperturbability of my personal judgment and personal direction of life; the autonomy of my decisions; the full acceptance and earnest practice of the inalienable responsibility which my life imposes upon me; and the "subjectivity of conscience," in the sense which Kierkegaard gives to that expression, viz., that I have appropriated the guiding truths and directives of my life and made them a part of my inner self, so that I do not think and live as a member of the crowd, or the impersonal "they" (*das Man*), as Heidegger was to say later.

5. FREE FROM AND FREE FOR

Let us now draw attention to a last dimension which has been constantly presupposed in our considerations. "Person" and "personality" designate an essentially ethical reality in man. One does not even have to touch the essence of the freedom just described if one considers it exclusively as a freedom of choice, a possibility to act or not to act in a particular situation, to do this or to do that.

The perennial dispute regarding freedom has nearly always been expressed in such terms that it seemed to be merely a psychological question. Could man also have refrained from action in a case where he did act? Could he also have acted differently where he acted in this particular way? The answers to such questions obviously are not subject to any exact, methodical verification. That is why a positivistic attitude of mind necessarily leads to a denial of freedom or at least an agnostic attitude toward it.

Freedom, however, is primarily a personal self-possession that is not simply given with manhood, but is rather a task and something to be acquired. Freedom, together with the obstacles that stand in its way, presents itself as something immediately evident in the immediate lived experience of the person who ascends to freedom in a constant struggle. Here especially, and most of all, the fundamental principle of existential phenomenology applies. Freedom is not "to be deduced or constructed" but "to be described" as something that presents itself in lived existence as belonging to our very way of existence itself. No subtle reasoning on the basis of biological or physical data can ever undermine that evidence because the very data upon which one then relies do not enjoy the immediate "givenness" with which freedom presents itself in self-conscious life. A complex reasoning process from the less known can never weaken the evidence with which the better known immediately presents itself. Moreover, all those reasonings start with a first categorial mistake by assuming that freedom is subject to examination by the methods of exact science. However, the consideration of freedom does not belong to the realm of knowledge to which exact science has access through its cognitive project and its methodical principles. While these principles constitute the strength of science, they also supply its limitations.

Freedom of choice is a property of our freedom in its incomplete realization: it is a by-product of genuine liberty. My tarrying in a particular situation can force me into a real situation of choice and puts before me the problem, "Should I or should I not? Should I act this way or that?" But this fact is a sign either of my lack of discernment in the situation, on account of which I do not recognize with certainty what my project is, or it is a sign of my inner lack of freedom, on account of which I do not dare to accept the project or feel unable to tackle it. As we have said above, however, perfect personality is characterized by unity of purpose. It does not have the single-mindedness of non-free nature but the single-mindedness, and hence predictability, of perfect freedom. The more free I am, the more the imperfection and ambiguity of choice disappear and the more purely also freedom appears to me as self-possession in the realization of the good. Hence the freedom of God contains nothing of the freedom of choice that is known to us by experience.

Freedom, when looked at and understood in this way, according to its true nature, reveals an ethical dimension which we must now try to explain clearly.

Personality and freedom, in the full sense of those terms, signify more than mere self-possession. For what is it that gives to life its orderly unity in the present and in time? What causes our powers to be harmoniously ordered at every moment? What makes us manifest the same orderly image of life from moment to moment, from day to day, year in, year out? Is it not a firm direction of our whole life to an ideal, to a supreme value of life? A man could be perfectly self-possessed and have enormous will-power but at the same time live a "disconnected" life, not because his passions cause that division, but through arbitrariness. As Stavrogin in Dostoevski's *Demons,* it could happen that a man does not know why he lives, to what he ought to devote his powers. He first tries one thing, then another. And the one appears to him as equally valuable or valueless as the other. As a young man once wrote to André Gide, "Master, I am free, I have freed myself. But free for what? This is the dreadful question!" Free for what? Only commitment gives meaning to freedom and firmness to a free life.

Accordingly that man is a true personality who possesses himself in freedom but who, at the same time, freely subjects himself to the highest value. Personality means two things: the highest accomplishment of human self-possession and the most firm self-commitment; inner independence and moral involvement; concentration in one's own hands and surrender to an ideal and a worthwhile task.

6. FREEDOM AND OBJECTIVE VALUE

What are the values for which self-possessing personality makes itself serviceable? There are subjective values that shape and nourish subjective life and there are objective values that establish and entertain objective life. In what do they differ? Reality has value for subjective life only as a source of biological satisfaction. This satisfaction of a biological need or impulse is a *subjective value*. The subjective activity, therefore, aims exclusively at the preservation, development, protection and perpetuation of the type of life proper to the subject. Hence the life of an animal is purely subjective. It lives exclusively on subjective values. An antelope has only food value for a hungry lion. When the lion is satisfied, the objective shape and grace of the antelope no longer interests him. There is no record of a hungry lion ever hesitating before the beauty of a gazelle, and saying, as it were, to himself, "How beautiful! Should I?"

One must be a man to venture out with a camera and brave a thousand dangers in order to film a rare animal in its natural environment. This is an objective interest, a being interested in reality for its own sake and not for some biological satisfaction, a finding of pure satisfaction in activities directed solely to the knowledge, the beauty, the welfare of objects and beings in a purely objective, disinterested and unselfish way. This kind of interest is proper to man alone on earth.

Accordingly, something has subjective value for me insofar as it satisfies my biological needs, and objective value insofar as the thing itself gives me satisfaction for itself, in its own inviolate objective existence. We can therefore say provisionally that a personality is someone who has sufficient control over the forces of his subjective life to be directed with his whole being to objective values. Those objective values are not abstract ideas or general ideals that loom up as a vague and unreal background behind concrete reality. Neither are they a transcendent world of imperishable Platonic forms mirrored in the shifting play of our perishable world. They are simply various ways in which reality itself, reality in and for itself, becomes a value for free self-conscious existence, that is, it becomes something in which the person discovers and experiences the meaningful fulfillment of his life.

He experiences that fulfillment of life in activities that are directed to reality as such. His conscious life is thereby united with reality in a communion which leaves reality intact. Those activities are pure, disinterested, unselfish, objective. We do not draw the other selfishly to ourselves, but turn disinterestedly to the other. They are not objects for our use, says St. Augustine, but are an object of *fruitio*. This untranslatable term can be approximated as finding the fulfillment of one's life and one's happiness in an activity of union with the objective reality of a being. It is the profound intuition that dawns also in the Thomistic definition of knowledge, "to possess the other as other," that is, without assimilating the other in any way into one's own organic life.

7. THE PERSON AS THE TRUE BEARER OF OBJECTIVE VALUE

All this is still too general and unsatisfactory. A further step in our reflection must lead us to the discovery that that objective value of reality properly belongs only to a person. It is only the person who has an inalienable value of purpose. The things that are below the level of personal existence have no real self-value, they have no intrinsic value of purpose. They belong to the realm of means, that which is the object of use, as St. Augustine expresses it.

The proper way in which non-personal reality presents itself in immediate experience, is as "at hand" (*vorhanden*), at our disposal; it is ready to be gotten hold of, ready to be used by us. To present itself in experience as "at hand" is the same as to offer only a purely useful value, a value of means. On the contrary, personal reality offers itself in immediate experience as a "presence." We discover the person before us as an inviting reality. The mere discovery of a reality as "present" is the discovery of its intrinsic and inviolable value. Father Martin d'Arcy beautifully describes how we "first discover others and salute them and address them as persons, as beings and persons who are most decidedly not ourselves, who demand of us that we treat them as beings who possess their own inalienable individuality and perfection. We are drawn to them not as being in any sense our own; it is just because they cannot be exploited or used or partitioned out that we attend to them, for what they are in themselves."[6]

An objective value is one that belongs to a reality in and for itself. Hence in the strict sense objective value belongs only to beings that enjoy the perfection of being in the strict sense. Now, being in the proper and true sense is substantial being. "Being" in the first and proper sense (*esse primum*) is that which constitutes the substance (*esse substantiale est esse primum*). That is why objective self-value belongs to a being only insofar as it realizes the value of substantiality. As we have already shown above, existence-in-itself or substantiality belongs properly speaking only to the person. This is the ultimate ontological reason why the only bearer of real objective self-value is the person. Hence the person is the sole being that can be the object of a spiritual act of communion.

However, it would be wrong to conclude that nature, that is, the material world insofar as it does not reach the level of personal existence, can be merely an object of exact research with a view to technico-utilitarian interventions. For non-personal nature is taken up into the world of the person; it loses all meaning if the presence of the person is removed from it in thought. The material world viewed in its total reality is the world of the person, the world in which the incarnate person realizes and discovers himself, and by which also the creative presence of God reveals itself to the person who lives on earth.

Hence nature is the medium through which the person expresses and reveals himself; it is therefore the means for living personal communications between incarnate persons and between these persons and their transcendent Creator. Nature, then, as a sign and symbol of a personal presence, as the outward manifestation of a personal reality, may be an object of disinterested contemplation and of activities of communion.

---

[6]Martin C. d'Arcy, *The Mind and the Heart of Love*, London, 1945, p. 321.

It would take us too far afield were we to go more deeply into this subject. Let us merely point out that that view we have just explained is not weakened by the fact that many mystics of nature experience a kind of enlargement of the soul in which it seems to them that they lose their personality and coincide with an all-being which they do not expressly experience and think of as personal reality. For the interpretation of experience does not always cover the actual content and meaning of that experience. Thus in the best-known witnesses of the mystical experience of nature, for instance, Alfred Tennyson, Forrest Reid, Warner Allen and R. Jefferies, we see clearly a certain doubt about the interpretation of their mystical experience. Tennyson for example, speaks of "the loss of personality (so it were) seeming no extinction but the only true life."[7] The loss of personality seems to mean rather that the isolation or closedness of the personality is broken through so that this personality seems to take in the all of things: "It was as if everything that had seemed to be external and around me were suddenly within me. The whole world seemed to be within me."[8] The falling away of the "I" is rather a falling away of the opposition between the "I" and the all-nature: "I was unaware of personality. I didn't think. . . . I was all consciousness, feeling awareness, but unconditioned, if 'I' could be called 'I' then."[9]

One gets the impression that it is not so much a question of the disappearance of the "I" into nature, than of nature being taken up into the "I." The mystic of nature experiences his way of existence in ecstacy as something paradoxical. This is described very well by Warner Allen: "I am absorbed in the Light of the Universe, in Reality glowing like fire, with the knowledge of itself, without ceasing to be one and myself, merged like a drop of quicksilver in the whole yet still separate like a grain of sand in the desert."[10] That ex-

---

[7]Letter to William James. Cf. W. James, *The Varieties of Religious Experience*, London, 1919, p. 384.

[8]Cf. Forrest Reid, *Following Darkness*, London, 1902, p. 42.

[9]From a letter of Dorothea Spinner; see R. C. Zaehner, *At Sundry Times*, London, 1958, p. 50.

[10]Warner Allen, *The Happy Issue*, London, 1948, p. 27.

perience is also brought out clearly in some of the ancient Indian *Upanishads,* where, for instance, in the *Kausitaki* (I, 6), the following dialogue takes place between the god Brahma and a deceased human being:

> Brahma: "Who art thou?"
> The Soul: "I am a season, connected with the seasons, produced from the womb of space . . . as the brilliance of the year and the soul of every being. You yourself are the soul of each thing. Who thou art, that am I."
> The Soul: "Who am I?"
> Brahma: "The Real."
> Brahma: "What is the Real?"
> The Soul: "It is co-extensive with this all.
>   This all art thou."

Pantheism too, when it is not merely a philosophical system but a living religion, moves in that ambiguity. Although the order of the world is described in impersonal terms, nevertheless, and contrary to all logic, it is treated as if it were governed by a personal Providence. This has often been seen in connection with Stoicism.[11] In Chinese Taoism we find the same phenomenon: "Tao has become the great all-controlling principle with something of the spark of personality in it."[12] Even the commentators of Spinoza not infrequently note a contradiction between the mystical experience on the basis of which Spinoza wrote, and the monistic closedness of his system. Most remarkable, however, is the development of ancient Indian thought in the *Upanishads.* We see there is a heroic struggle of the mind desiring to grasp the nature of the source from which all things have arisen. And it cannot be denied that first in the *Katha* and the *Mundaka,* and finally with full clarity in the *Svetasvatara,* the fundamental source takes in the features of a transcendent Creator. The famous "Song of the Blessed One,"

---

[11]"However non-Stoical it may be . . ., Zeus acquires the figure of a personal God and becomes the *Pronoia,* a good providence full of care for the world and men." (A Henderickx, in *Theologisch Woordenboek,* Vol. III, 1958, col. 4427).

[12]Karl L. Reichelt, *Religion in Chinese Garment,* Tr. by J. Tetlie, London, 1951, p. 80.

the *Bhagavad-Gita,* later took up that whole struggle and attained to the recognition of a God who desires to enter into a communion of love with men.[13]

8. UNITY OF THE CULTURAL ACTIVITIES IN THE ETHICAL DIMENSION

As we have seen, the person does not realize and fulfill his being a person in solitary self-possession but in the activities of communion with the real as such. We have specified with what reality the person must enter into communion in order to realize himself: it is the reality of the person, which is reality in its full and proper sense. Like the objects to which the communion is directed, the activities by which we exercise this communion now must also be reduced to a unity. For these too are not a plurality of independent actions, of cognitive, aesthetic and ethical acts. In their final meaningful coherence they constitute together one activity, and this activity is an ethical one. True, a careful phenomenological reflection distinguishes diverse activities according to the abstract diversity of their natures; but considered concretely and existentially, each activity that is objectively directed to reality itself is an expression of personal freedom and, hence, is ethical in its most profound foundation. As Newman said already, authentic thought and assent is a free, ethical activity in which the person as a whole is involved.

Due to our power of abstraction, we can fix our attention on the world of nature insofar as it is "at hand" as a purely useful value. In this way we make nature the object of various natural sciences and techniques. But then we do not direct our attention to the real precisely in respect to its proper character as reality, for as soon as our mind aims at reality, we enter the realm of the ethical. Moreover, every abstraction, even that which gives rise to natural science and technology, finally needs to be taken up again in an ethical

---

[13]For the preceding section I am particularly indebted to the two works of Prof. R. C. Zaehner of Oxford, *Mysticism, Sacred and Profane,* Oxford, 1957, and *At Sundry Times,* London, 1958.

attitude toward the proper, that is, the personal reality. It follows that the use of science and technique must be controlled by the ethical demands of the personal community. Science and technology are means in the service of the personal life of man, and this life always remains the end. To endanger the well-being of the human community of persons by sacrificing man to the development of technology for its own sake would destroy the tissues of the social organism like a cancer.

This statement must not be interpreted as a condemnation of modern technological progress. This progress can be of great service for the well-being of the community of persons, but on condition that we retain the fundamental idea that the use of those means must be strictly subordinated to the ethical demands of the human community. No doubt, it is due to the profound and universal influence of personalism that the principle that science and technology must be in the service of man has become one of the leading ideas in our present day world.

9. UNITY OF THE ETHICAL ACTIVITY IN LOVE

Thus the whole activity by which man is busy in a human way in the realm of means is in principle taken up into a higher activity. By this activity men form a community of persons, that is, a community in which they attain for one another an inalienable value of ends to be striven for in a disinterested way. That higher activity, however, must itself be reduced to a unity. In all its pursuits that higher activity must be the expression of a fundamental ethical attitude. This fundamental ethical attitude is love.

Love contains in itself the whole ethical way of existence in which the person attains a true self-realization and self-fulfillment. Love is nothing but the objectivity of self-conscious life, the disinterestedness of the fundamental human will: a consent to, and acceptance and service of, that which truly *is*. As we have seen, it is only the person that *is* in the true and strict sense. Love is the original choice by which human existence is directed to the real as such. From this fundamental attitude evolves man's whole authentic life, not only in his ethical conduct, but also in his thought and in the aesthetic act which is an intuitive contemplation of the mystery of things in the form in which they appear.

It is only through love and sympathy that we penetrate into reality itself, that is, to the personal core, which is the secret of all that exists. To express it paradoxically, by love our life attains that objectivity by which we enter into a conscious spiritual communion with the subjectivity of another person. By love the superficial relation between the abstractly knowing subject and an abstract object of knowledge is overcome and is taken up into the full concrete relation of a knowing person with and to a known person.

Martin Buber called the latter relation an "I-thou" relation in contrast with the relation of "I" to "it" or "him." He thought, however, that such knowledge no longer shows the structure of a subject-object relation. We are in full sympathy with his concern to distinguish clearly the proper nature of a conscious communication between persons from the neutral relation of the mind to an object of purely scientific investigation. Nevertheless, his analysis remains somewhat superficial. In our human existence a subject can be known only by becoming an object for us. Hence the personal way of knowing must use the phenomenal object as an indispensable medium in order to reach the other subject. Here, undoubtedly, we are confronted with a "shifting of meaning" in the terms. "Objectivity," in the sense of knowledge of reality itself, is attained only when, passing through the "objective" (in the sense of what appears before us), we penetrate to the personal core, which is genuine reality. In our human way of knowing, perfect objectivity which touches the reality itself can never be totally divested of the other, imperfect objectivity by which being can be known by us only in something that "appears" and can be grasped as a "representation." Even the mystic, who in his higher states of consciousness is temporarily freed from all

representation, constantly falls back on the human foundation of "representative" consciousness from which he must
always start again in order to immerse himself in that which
cannot be represented.

We see, then, that love stands at the beginning and the
end of all true activity in which man attains the perfection
of personality. It is the fundamental attitude from which
life unfolds, not only in action but also in thought and in
the creation of forms. It is at the same time the crowning
act in which both the life of knowledge and that of the contemplation and creation of forms culminate and in which
they fulfill their meaning. That crowning act consists in
"being a man for others," to use the felicitous expression
with which Dietrich Bonhoeffer designated the exemplary
human value of Christ. To love is to experience the meaning
of our existence and find our happiness in activities that
are directed disinterestedly to the personal well-being of
others. To accept another person as a value, for his own
sake, to put myself unselfishly at the service of his personal
unfolding and the perfecting of his being, and to find in
this service a pure and profound joy and happiness, this is
love.

Accordingly, love inwardly unfolds itself in the attitude—
twofold and yet profoundly one—of goodwill that is objectively directed to the other (*amor benevolentiae*) and of a
complacency that comes to rest objectively in the other
(*amor complacentiae*). When love is mutual it gives rise to
the highest form of personal communion. If it is intimate, on
the basis of a shared life, it develops into a friendship.

10. Summary and Conclusion

In summation, that which is proper to a person and
finds its fulfillment in personality, cannot be defined exclusively as "self-possession." A complete definition should
read "self-possession within an objectively directed project
of life." The closedness of self-possession has meaning only
through openness to objective life. That to which the activi-

ties of the objective project of life are directed is ultimately the personal world in which being-real finds its proper realization. In this way we ultimately arrive at "personal community" as the unitary formula which defines the object of the activity making the person. This activity itself can be summed up in the word "love." Love, then, which creates the personal community is the proper perfection of personality. Hence, self-possession, or freedom in the true sense of the word, cannot be defined as freedom of arbitrariness, that is, freedom of doing what one wants. It must be determined as ethical freedom, in other words, as a freedom to do what one ought to do, as a freedom to respond completely and without impediment to the invitation that the very discovery of the person implies for us.

In conclusion, we want to point out once more that the ethical metaphysics of the person described in this chapter makes no claims to being a complete metaphysical theory of value. The thoughts we have developed were placed within a definite perspective and could also have been examined from a different standpoint. No view of reality can claim to disclose the whole of reality. We have developed our view here within the perspective of our existence in the world as being in search of ultimate meaning. This perspective led us to affirm that neither nature, the realm of necessity, nor culture, the realm of conquered freedom, represent an ultimate satisfactory value, but that both are completely directed to the community of persons which is the kingdom of love. Only in this kingdom do nature and culture attain their true character of value.

Our dynamic reflection from the standpoint of man in search of meaning does not exclude the possibility that created reality can be seen metaphysically also in its immediate relation to the creative source. The whole kingdom of creation will then present itself as a manifold reflection and manifestation of the simple uncreated Goodness from which all things proceed. Looked at within the whole order of creation, as a reflection of a creating Goodness, every being,

115

every aspect, every part, every acquisition makes its own irreducible contribution to the value and significance of the whole.

Nevertheless, that contemplative view must also take account of the fact that the value of the divine manifestation ultimately belongs to the development of God's work of creation as a whole. The universal all-embracing order, and it alone, manifests in a true and complete sense the goodness of its first origin. That whole is precisely ordered by the Creator to be a revelation of His goodness. This revelation begins in unconscious nature and appears with gradually increasing clarity in the order of created beings until it manifests itself fully in the vocation of the created person to a community of persons and finally—since God's entire work is one—to a community of salvation. In this way both considerations meet in a higher synthesis.

CHAPTER SIX

PERSONALISM: THE PERSONALISTIC COMMUNITY

1. Introductory Remarks

Following its own line of development, our metaphysics of the person has unfolded into an ethics of personal existence. At the same time, by making us enter the realm of personal ethics, this development has led us to the domain of the community. This aspect we must now develop further.

At the end of the previous chapter we entered the house, as it were, through the skylight, that is, the idea of the human community impressed itself on our mind first in its highest ideal form, as a unity in love of distinct and independent personalities. That community has the value of a purpose in which the person attains his perfect realization and fulfillment. On that highest level the good of the community and the good of the person coincide. Realized person is identical here with realized community. The value of the person is realized and actualized in the measure in which the community of love has become a reality. Considered in itself on that highest level, there is no distinction between common good and private good, for love precisely makes the good and well-being of the others be the personal good of the lover.

Before developing that idea and analyzing more fully the form of unity proper to the community that has been established in that way, we must come down from those heights and begin this time from the bottom. In doing this, however, we must keep in mind that, as we have shown, a community animated by love must be the aim of our whole personal existence. All human relations therefore must ultimately be integrated into that community in order to find therein their ultimate meaning and justification.

A person is a whole and it is also as such that he forms a community with others: not merely as a biological entity, not merely as a mind, but as a human whole. He is completely taken up into the community both as a subject and as an object of the activities that form the community. For the person as a whole is involved in the community and, at the same time, its end. This human whole, however, can be looked at in various ways, viz., as an individual, as a person and as a personality.

2. THE INDIVIDUAL AND THE ECONOMIC COMMUNITY

Man is an individual of the human species. In virtue of his birth he comes into the world as a product of nature, a typical living organism that depends for its existence, growth and sustenance on the material goods offered by the environment. It is a well-known fact that man's material needs are greater than those of other living organisms. For example, the need to protect his body by clothes and shelter makes heavy demands and these demands become more exacting as man advances in civilization. Also, much more than other animals, man is dependent on the members of his species for the satisfaction of his bodily needs. He is helpless and in need of the care of others for a much longer time. All these things which man needs to preserve his bodily life and satisfy his biological needs constitute together the domain of man as an individual.

This consideration of the individual reveals a first aspect of man's sociability. He is dependent on others for the care of his bodily existence and this dependence has its counterpart in the help human beings give one another in these matters. This mutual dependence and aid suffice to give rise to a kind of community, a relational whole of which the individuals are members because of their bodily existence. This economic aspect of the community manifests itself very clearly in the bond of the family and the tribe. As the world develops, however, the economic whole on which man depends becomes increasingly larger. In our time it tends to become world-wide; today our bodily well-being is dependent on events that occur on the other side of the earth.

Accordingly, there is a fundamental respect in which the human community is an economic community. The activities by which the community is formed in that respect are in certain cases of immediate assistance, for instance, the help given to children by their parents, still somewhat rooted in instinct, although even then they are no longer instinctive activities in the true sense of the word. Economic activities in the strict sense are the work of human reason. Reason endeavors to produce and distribute with ever greater order and efficiency the goods that are necessary for the bodily life of man.

This general reference to the economic dimension of man must suffice. We know, of course, that economy is not directed solely to the production and distribution of goods that serve man's bodily life. It also aims at the production and distribution of goods that serve the higher life of the person. But everything cannot be said at once. We must begin with the consideration of the economy in function of those basic goods that are necessary for man's corporal life.

3. THE RIGHT OF OWNERSHIP

It is important for our investigation to realize at once that individuality is but one aspect of the human whole or person. The body is not an independent part of man, but man's bodiliness is something of the person. By his body the human person exists in the world, which is the domain of his life. He cannot live without his body. Through his bodiliness, "the joined instrument" of higher activities, man fulfills his vocation in this world and is able to fashion himself into a personality. Without the body we cannot do anything, we cannot think, nor contemplate, will nor work.

As a consequence the individual bodiliness, taken up into the unity of the person, partakes also of the inviolability of the person. The human person must be fully respected by others in regard to his bodily component. Once he has entered this world as a person, he has an inalienable right to existence, to the integrity and health of his body and to

119

everything that is necessary to sustain his body and give it a wholesome development. He has a right to sustenance of life and to the means to acquire the things necessary for it.

This, of course, is a very general principle. It is impossible to go into all the problems that are connected with every point in this discussion. Let us merely emphasize the fact that, because man's bodily existence depends on his having access to the goods of life offered by the natural environment, the inviolable right to corporeal existence and bodily care implies, by that very fact, that he has the right to call certain things his own. They are his and they belong to him. This principle is the firm and lasting foundation of the right of ownership. For, to own something means to have something as my own and to be able to dispose of it in such a way that others may not deprive me of it. Man has an inalienable right of ownership because he is a person.

This formula, too, is still very general and must be properly understood. The right of ownership, as it follows by strict logic from the nature of man's embodied personal existence in his earthly environment, means only that man has a right guaranteeing him whatever he needs for his sustenance. But all men have that fundamental right since being a person is the fundamental title on which the right of ownership is based. That is why all additional titles, such as inheritance and work, are subject to the requirements of the first and essential foundation of the right. They must yield where the fundamental right of others has a claim. The right of private ownership and of increase in ownership has a limit based on the natural law, namely, the right of others to possess a guarantee for their existence.

If someone through inheritance and successful economic enterprises were to become the owner of the whole world, he would not have the right to say: "All this belongs to me and I do with it what I will. I let others live from it, not because they have a right to it, but for other reasons such as humanitarian feelings or love of neighbor." From his right would have to be subtracted at least everything that is required to safeguard the bodily security of all others. What applies to this utopian case is true also with respect to great fortunes in a partial community here on earth. It is the duty of the community and its leaders to take measures for a just distribution of earthly goods, that is, a distribution according to the demands of each person's fundamental right.

It is also evident that the realization of the right of ownership, that is, the right of the person to possess a guarantee for his use of the goods needed for life, will lead to additional demands according to the economic and social development of our world. Where people live together in small, very closed economic units, the right of ownership is the inviolable right of disposing of their small economic domain and everything belonging to it: their house, their land, their tools, meadows, etc. But where economic relations have developed further, the concrete demands of the right of ownership also change their patterns in accordance with the general economic situation. Industrial development can widen the economic whole within which man lives and on which he depends and can create a large national economy. It can fundamentally change the techniques of economic production. In such a case the demands of the right of ownership change at the same time. The right to work and to a just remuneration for work done then comes to the fore, and the right of the individuals to see their possessions respected by others gradually develops into some forms of positive care excercised by the community and by those charged with its welfare.

At present the economic whole on which human life depends is beginning to encompass the entire world, and taking care of man on a world-wide scale will sooner or later become a possibility. The logical conclusion must now be drawn that the less developed human groups and those that are particularly threatened in their bodily existence have the right to aid and support from more developed and affluent nations. This is not a matter of world charity but of world justice.

121

With this conclusion we are already turning from man, as the object of activities that respect the inviolability of his individual necessities of life, to man as the ethical subject of such activities. According to the first consideration, he is a person who has rights; according to the second, he is a person who is just or acts justly. A just action is one that gives to another what belongs to him, what is due to him, what he has a right to. The virtue of justice is the firm moral attitude by which man, as a matter of course, acts in accordance with the right of others. This point cannot yet be fully developed here, for it is not solely in the bodily sphere of life that right and justice excercise their rule. We shall return to it presently.

4. Person and Cultural Community

Secondly, the human whole can be considered as a person. This person must be seen from the start as directed to personality. For personality is the successful realization of what being a person contains as a task and a vocation. Yet, precisely as such a task, man is particularly dependent upon others and in need of their help.

Man, as we have shown in the previous chapter, is a project and task for himself. He must laboriously try to reach the human height of inner freedom. This task presupposes first of all a certain understanding, not only of the world of passions and emotions that affect him interiorly, but also of the situation in which he finds himself, viz., the world of nature and of man. He needs above all an understanding of the ultimate meaning of the world and the life he must lead in it. He must also know clearly the motives that can inspire and guide his life. His personal self-becoming implies, moreover, training for the methodical acquisition of a great number of intellectual and moral achievements by which man attains self-possession and control over life.

It is evident that man needs the help of others if he wishes to acquire understanding of life and self-control. Although the work this involves can be achieved only by himself and through his personal efforts—all education is ultimately self-education—he will not be successful without outside help. No one, left to himself, can by his own powers obtain the insights which mankind has acquired only through many centuries of great effort. No one can by his own solitary experience find the correct and suitable ways for self-formation which the experience of the whole of mankind has discovered only slowly and through many detours and errors. A successful realization of the task implied in being a person can be attained only by a careful initiation into the tradition of the historical, self-thinking life of mankind. To introduce and initiate others into the tradition of culture is the active task of the educator.

By their mutual assistance for the attainment of full human dignity men form a community, a new kind of relational whole. We can call such a community a community of culture. The expression, however, is not entirely adequate because culture, as we shall see, extends also to the economic transformation of the world. Nevertheless, since human excellence is the true end and meaning of economic prosperity in the same way as the person is the end and meaning of the body, we may apply the term "cultural community" in a specific way to the relational whole constituted by those activities aiming at the cultivation of human excellence, and we may distinguish it as such from the economic community. Within the cultural community, men are united in a tradition of culture which they support, transmit and cause to advance.

Within the cultural community every person has the right to education, that is, to sufficient and suitable initiation in the spiritual treasures and acquisitions of cultures. Just as man has the right to a firm guarantee of access to the material goods that are necessary for his bodily existence and welfare, so also has he the right to get from others and the community the necessary access to the goods of the objective culture of the mind, and to receive a firm guarantee in their regard. This right implies that, in accordance with its degree of

123

economic and spiritual development, the means required for a good initiation in the objective tradition of culture must be developed by the community for the benefit of its members to the best of its possibilities. Such means are schools and libraries, buildings and other facilities for worship, institutions for recreational activities and particular forms of education, and at the same time the possibility for everyone to enjoy all those things according to his needs and abilities.

Accordingly, it is necessary to admit a certain development of the implications contained in the fundamental right to education. The practical demands of justice expressing that fundamental right in the concrete conditions of society are not the same in a primitive community and in a highly developed cultural community. In the former, life is encompassed by the family or tribe, but in the latter, man participates in the broader life of a nation which has the means to develop the institutions necessary for education and self-formation. In this area also the right of the person no longer involves a claim only on those persons to whom the care of his education is immediately entrusted. It involves more and more the responsibility of the community as a whole and hence of those who are charged with the care of the nation. Moreover, we have now entered a period in which mankind is becoming one world and thinking in terms of world-wide culture and economy. We must therefore be prepared to take on the responsibility of providing what is required for the education of all mankind.

5. Unity of the Economic Community and the Cultural Community

Our investigation has made us discover two levels of existence on which man constitutes a community with his fellow-men. As a bodily individual, he depends on the members of his species for the secure satisfaction of his biological needs. That is why he forms an economic community which applies itself to the development and organization of the material means for the bodily well-being of all. As a person, that is, as a self-project directed to a higher form of humanity, man is dependent on the members of his species for a good education and a suitable initiation in the cultural tradition. As such, he is taken up into a cultural community in which the members, by manifold activities, by intentional or unintentional, direct or indirect communications, exercise a formative influence upon one another. Before going on to the third and highest consideration of the human community, let us make a synthesis of the first two.

The economic community and the cultural community compenetrate each other and form an organic unity. The distinction of various fields or levels should not mislead us; not reality itself but our way of looking at things makes us distinguish them. As we have already suggested above, economic activities are not directed exclusively to the rational production and distribution of the earthly goods necessary for our biological activities. They are also directed to the organization and diffusion of the objective cultural goods which man needs in order to fulfill properly his personal human vocation. We should now see clearly what this means.

On the other hand, culture affects not only the person but also the environment. Culture is the ensemble of the structures which man calls forth from nature by his creative thought and his efforts. Hence culture encompasses the economic as well as the personal and social acquisitions of our earthly existence. This existence is truly an existence in the world (*"in-der-Welt-sein"*). Our pursuit of existence is directed to and dependent on the world in which we find ourselves. This world is not merely a world around us (an *Umwelt*), a world we live on to sustain our bodily life; but it is also an open world, spread before us (*Welt*), a world in which we discover and realize ourselves by unveiling and realizing meanings in it. The humanization of our own being and the humanization of our world, the spiritualization of our consciousness and the spiritualization of our milieu go hand in hand. Hence, self-possession and possession of the world, self-control and control over the earth, asceticism and technology form a unity. Together they constitute the self-possession of human life that encompasses both the world and the person in his pursuit of existence.

Through the synthesis of those two aspects of community we obtain the concept of a community directed to a goal which embraces our bodily welfare as well as our personal self-fulfillment and in which the economy plays the role of a servant and creator of means for both purposes. Thus we discover within that unity a definite structure of ends and means. The meaning of culture is the liberation of man. Achieving freedom with respect to the outside world by the technological control of matter is directed toward achieving freedom with respect to the inner world through acquiring self-control in the life of the spirit. The purpose of economic development is not confined to making the earth serve man, but it is ultimately destined to make him free from being absorbed by that work of making the earth serve his needs. This liberation will always be incomplete and partial. However, our time, which witnesses the rapid development of automation, has opened perspectives that clearly indicate how technological progress can free man more and more from bondage to work and economic requirements.

Freedom for what? This is the problem. The theoretical answer is evident: to be free for a more intense and higher culture of the person. But the practical answer rests in the hands of modern man. It depends upon him whether he will recognize the higher values that invite him to the culture of the person and whether he will become so deeply engaged in them that he will resist the temptation to inertia and the superficiality of sense life.

6. PERSONALITY AND PERSONAL COMMUNITY

The highest values which give meaning to man's whole existence are values of the spiritual community of persons. We have now reached again the summit from which, at the beginning of this chapter, we entered the realm of human community; but we now look at that community on the level of the realized personality. This realization includes everything we have considered before. Just as the material freedom of existence is directed to ethical freedom of self-possession and attains in it the fulfillment of its human meaning, so is the latter totally directed to community of persons in a union of love. Only in this union is the human meaning ultimately achieved.

The personal community is a direct community of life that binds person to person. Within this community the other person has no longer the value of a means to help me satisfy my biological needs in the best way possible, or to help me discern the road that will lead me to true self-possession. The other person now acquires the value of an end and purpose. I attain my genuine self-fulfillment only when I am lovingly oriented to the total personal good of the other and devote my life to this good. I thus enter into communion with the other in a most unique way. It is no longer a question of a common participation in a material or a spiritual good, but of a communion by participation in the good that the other himself is. In other words, it is not a community of *having* but a community of *being*.

In this community of being we acquire the highest, the definitive kind of freedom: not a being-free from the bonds in which surrounding nature holds us, not a being-free from the bonds in which our own nature constrains us; but a being-free from the bond of our own self, a liberation from the solitariness and the limitations in which self-love detains us. This freedom means an expansion of our being, a loosening of the chains that keep us fettered to our own heart. Thus our pursuit of personal existence now extends to the other and ultimately to the all-embracing whole which, as we have seen, is, in its inmost mystery, a personal reality. Through love we are our own selves, and are with ourselves, in the other. The center of our life is no longer our own separate personal core but it is equally the personal core of the others. The center of our existence coincides, in a perfect freedom of love, with that of the whole of reality. By love, our existence is directed to the good of the whole and our own good coincides with the universal good. This point needs to be understood properly. We must therefore objectively consider all the problems and difficulties which arise from that statement and attempt clear answers to them.

7. THE NATURE OF LOVE

Several factors make it difficult to philosophize about love. First of all, our language is a language of things; hence the meaning of our words is always more or less metaphorical when we speak about the mystery of the person and especially about the deepest mystery of the person, which is love. Secondly, a philosophical study of love leads us into a world of puzzles that can find an intelligible and satisfactory solution only in terms of the revealed mystery. For a person, love should be the most natural thing in the world and yet it is too conspicuously absent from this world. Self-love apparently cannot be overcome by any human effort. Liberation through love always appears as a kind of miracle, a grace, a mysterious conversion. Of this the philosopher cannot give a satisfactory explanation. He can in the end do nothing but listen with understanding to the message that says: "Imprisoned by sin, saved by grace." To which he should then answer: "This would be an acceptable solution indeed, although I am not able to prove it."

A first philosophical problem arises from the inner paradox of love itself. Love is really directed to the other for himself. Hegel has expressed this idea in a beautiful way: "Love is to forget oneself in an other self, but to have and possess oneself only in that disappearing and forgetting."[1] The spiritual act of love is directed to the other and not to one's own "I." But precisely in that pure orientation to the other, the lover acquires his highest personal perfection. "He who loses his life

---

[1]"Sich in einem anderen Selbst zu vergessen, doch in diesem Vergehen und Vergessen sich erst selber zu haben und zu besitzen." Hegel, *Aesthetik*, II, *Werke* (Glockner, ed.), vol. XIII, p. 149.

will gain it." This evangelical paradox expresses something that belongs to the nature of all true love. Love is my perfection, but I attain that perfection in the other. It is only by way of the other as other that love returns to me.

In love, I attain my highest personal self-realization, even when that love is unfortunate, that is, when it finds no response. Nothing can deprive the true lover of that highest perfection of being which he acquires in and by the act of love. Suffering love or crucified love is perfect love and therefore makes the lover, the subject of the act of love, perfect. The example of Christ who died, totally abandoned, reveals the nature of all authentic love. To this idea we must hold unconditionally. Otherwise, all our speaking about love will contain a contradiction; and we will confuse matters that are so strongly opposed to one another that it would be absurd to use the same term for all.

The well-known saying that orderly love begins with oneself can be interpreted in such a way that it is reduced to a trivial bourgeois slogan. True love for oneself is not opposed to love for others, but coincides with it. My highest good is love and this love is essentially directed to the other. That is why if I truly love myself, I shall desire for myself this highest good, namely, that of losing myself in the other. To the extent that the lover does something for his own benefit to the detriment of his love for the other, he falls short of pure love. True love begins with oneself because love, though totally directed to the other, cannot be anything but the highest self-perfection that I must desire for myself.

There exists a famous controversy about "pure love," that is, the idea that love must be so unselfish that it desires no enrichment through the encounter. This controversy, however, rests ultimately on a misunderstanding, for both parties start from the dilemma: Either I desire the other as my perfection and happiness, or I desire the other at the expense of my own perfection and happiness. This dilemma is false, for it is precisely in the absolute disinterestedness of "pure love" that the highest perfection and the purest happiness consists.

The purer my love for the other, the more do I attain my own perfection.

The attention, however, of the lover in the act of love is not directed to his own perfection and happiness, but to the good of the other. Love for the other can never be degraded so as to become a means for my own perfection. There is here no relationship of end and means. When I love, I am with myself in the other, and I become perfect in willing his perfection. Objective knowledge of something other than myself is likewise a perfection for me; yet the intentional act of my knowing is not, on that account, directed to knowledge as my own perfection but is directed to the thing known. So also is love my supreme perfection, but the intention of the will to love is not directed to my own perfection but to the other.

Here is an example of the great danger which threatens us because of the fact that, when we reflect on the mystery of the person, we make use of certain ideas and images that are borrowed from the non-personal world. "Every being strives for perfection." This is a metaphysical insight. But when we think of it, we use images that are spontaneously borrowed from the biological realm. A plant, an organism, by a natural tendency strives for its own development and self-realization and for the preservation and propagation of its own kind of life. Aristotle, in fact, conceived this principle in a purely naturalistic way. However, in the light of the discovery of the person in Christian philosophy, its application must be so differentiated that the radical opposition between nature and person comes to light. Because the perfection of the person lies in the perfect disinterestedness of love, a person's striving for perfection is a going out to the other as such in self-forgetfulness.

8. LOVE AND RETURN OF LOVE

Now that we have grasped and understood love in its pure essence, we can look at it also from the other side. Undoubtedly, love asks for a return of love, it cannot help asking for such a return. By its very essence, love involves an invitation. For it desires the personal good of the other and this good cannot lie in anything else than that the other would also become a lover. In this way also, God's most pure love wills that we return His love so that we too may attain to perfect love. Only through the other's return of love is our love freed from the pain of incompleteness and unfulfillment. This unfulfillment does not affect our own act of love, but it concerns the realization of its object; the perfection of the other which our love desires and for which it strives. So long as the other does not attain the perfection which our love wills to attain in the other, our love suffers pain in its "other" just as an organism suffers pain in one of its members.

It is only by a return of love that the communion comes about, the perfect community of persons in which the lovers are completely themselves and at home in one another. The fact that in this world true love appears mostly as a crucified love is based on the mystery of sin. But the cross is the way to glorification in the all-fulfilling communion of God's love. However, in saying this, we leave the domain of philosophy and enter that of theology. As we have already said, only the revealed mystery can give us the ultimate solution of our philosophical puzzles, but the philosopher can recognize this truth.

Of course, we are not pure spirits. We exist in the world of men through our body, and we work in the world by making use of material means. There are cases in which love can demand that we sacrifice our possessions and even life itself. We are not permitted, however, to cast either of them away frivolously. We continue to bear the responsibility for our life and our belongings. We have been called into this world by God's love to work in it for His kingdom by means of our love. We would be unfaithful to the loving intention of God if we wantonly deprived the human world of our presence and ceased working for His kingdom.

9. THE UNITY OF THE COMMUNITY OF PERSONS

It follows that the human community, in its highest form and on the level of perfectly realized personality, is pure intersubjectivity in mutual love. We must now determine the nature of the unity that characterizes this kind of community. Let us insist once more, however, that the intersubjectivity in question is the value in which the person realizes and achieves his being a person as such. That is why this intersubjectivity is also the end and goal to which the cultural community, together with all its activities, is ultimately directed. In the intersubjectivity of love every human community finds its true meaning, its fulfillment, hence also its ultimate foundation and justification. The loving community of persons summarizes and encompasses in itself the whole reality of the human community. For this reason the mode of its unity unqualifiedly determines also the metaphysical nature of the human community. As Aristotle already said, "the first definition is made by the end." This is particularly true of man, who can be understood and therefore properly defined only by the end which he is called to attain.

Man is said to be "the image of God." According to St. Thomas, this expression defines not the nature with which man begins to exist, but the end to which he is called in virtue of his being a person. "The image of God" defines man much more realistically then Aristotle's "rational animal," for the latter defines man statically according to the manner of being with which he, by nature, begins his existence. For the same reason the true metaphysical nature of our social existence must be defined as an intersubjective community of persons.

The personal community is a relational whole of which persons are parts insofar as they are self-existent wholes. They are not members of that community according to some part of themselves or in some respect; but they are parts with their whole self. That is why we may apply here the metaphysical principle that the part is for the sake of the whole. This principle is valid here in a most perfect way.

Man exists for the community. The being of the person is in a certain sense a being-for (*esse ad*) or relation, and the term of the relation that constitutes him is the community.

The highest theological model of that unity of the personal community is the Blessed Trinity in which the Persons are totally constituted by their relation to one another. They thus form an intersubjective unity which is not, as Gilbert de la Porrée wrongly imagined, something superadded to the concrete unity of the nature of God, but identical with it and in a mysterious way constitutes it. The second theological model is that of the Mystical Body in which by grace and love we form the body, or the one person, of the "whole Christ." These models supplied by faith should encourage the Christian philosopher in his endeavor to analyze the intimate unity of the personal community along the logical lines of his own personalistic principles, to envision it as a "whole man" of which the different persons are parts and, as it were, members. In the personal community of full intersubjectivity we form one body of love.

All men, says St. Thomas, in a certain sense form one man.[2] By this he undoubtedly means something more than the abstract unity of the species or of the biological unity of our descent from one man. A concrete spiritual unity of the community is meant in which the possibilities of one concrete manhood are fulfilled. It is true that St. Thomas confines himself to a summary declaration of the general analogy between the relation of the body to its many members and that of "man" to the many persons who are members of it. However, his theological use of that idea can be most fruitful when we make the analogy explicit and clearly bring out the essential difference between the functional unity of the organism and the spiritual unity of the community of persons. Undoubtedly, the community spoken of by St. Thomas is more than the personal community of intersubjectivity, inso-

---

[2]*In III Sent.*, dist. 18, a. 6, sol. 1, *Quodlib.* VII, a. 17; *In Epist. ad Rom.*, cap. V. lect. 3; *Summa contra Gentiles,* IV, 52; *Summa Theol.*, p. I-II, q. 81, a. 1; *Comp. Theol.*, 196.

133

far as the philosopher can speak about it, for it ultimately refers to the Mystical Body of Christ. The human community of persons is taken up into that Mystical Body by grace and perfected by it, although the philosopher is unable to establish this. He meets here the same difficulty as in the life of grace. He cannot penetrate into that life either, although, as we saw at the end of Chapter Three, it is in the life of grace that our manhood is interiorly brought to fullness.

The affirmation that the whole of the person is a part of the community and is therefore entirely directed to the community as to his end, does not destroy the absolute and inviolable end-value of the individual person himself. On the contrary, the fundamental principle remains true that the person realizes and fulfills his own end-value in the community-building act by which he aims at the other for the other himself. Within the community of persons, all persons are ends for one another. The perfect community is the realization of the end-value of all its members, but precisely by their being mutually connected in a disinterested way. A community realized is a person realized (*societas in actu est persona in actu*). It is true that the perfect identity of realized person and realized community is to be found only in their perfect achievement. But, as we have said, the best definition of a being is its definition by the end or ideal perfection to which it is destined or called. The proper end of a being reveals most clearly its essence. Hence the person is just as much the end of society as society is the end of the person. Those two statements merely express two aspects of one and the same reality.

The loving community of persons is also a community of perfect freedom, for a community of love can be formed only through that which constitutes the fundamental core of personality, namely, freedom. Love never forces things; violence is in contradiction with the essence of love. To try to force someone in any way to a community of love is a contradiction in terms. Love begs, calls, invites and appeals to the other's freedom, but compulsion would falsify its intention. Compulsion is also foreign to the love of God. Precisely for this reason the possibility of damnation, of self-chosen eternal death and isolation, is a possibility that follows from the very essence of God, who is love. This is the reason also why the thesis that grace absolutely respects the freedom of the human person is an essential thesis of Christianity with its belief that God is essentially love.

The community of love is not identified with the family, the nation, or any particular form of society but tends to realize itself in every form. It transcends every concrete form of coexistence and yet is immanent in all. It permeates the fundamental forms of human coexistence, such as the family, the circle of friends, and the nation. As an ideal to be attained it is active in everyone of those concrete forms of coexistence and wants to raise them to a form of unity in which service and mutual recognition of freedom is realized most perfectly: "Men and women in society are always looking for a closer unity of friendship and love, which protects and fosters distinction of personality as well as plurality."[3] Accordingly, the personal community is the ultimate aim pursued by every community, however tragic may be the failures caused by our sinful pride. The personal community is for the philosopher the salvation, the "making whole," of the person in a communion of love which creates the whole, the metaphysical unity of the community.

Hegel says this in his own characteristic way: "Union as such is itself the true content and purpose, and the destiny of individuals is that of leading a general life."[4] It is astonishing how this extraordinary thinker, who is so deeply rooted in his Christian past, but who distorted Christianity in his philosophical system, nevertheless explains so perfectly the deepest and most authentic ideas of Christianity whenever he considers such ideas independently of his

---

[3]Martin C. d'Arcy, *The Meeting of Love and Knowledge,* London, 1958, p. 65.
[4]"Die Vereinigung als solche ist selbst der wahrhafte inhalt und Zweck, und die Bestimmung der Individuen ist ein allgemeines Leben zu führen." Hegel, *Philosophie des Rechtes, Werke* (Glockner, ed.) Vol. VII, p. 129.

system. Hegel also very clearly expressed the fundamental personalistic view stating that the person is the absolute end of society just as society is the absolute end of the person. That is why he affirmed the divine character or absolute value of the family and of the state, of the Church and of the philosophical community of minds. This shows that for him also none of those forms is identical with the personal community, but that man in each one of them is looking for a community which transcends them all.[5]

It is precisely in this that we, Christians, differ from Hegel. According to him, the earthly community of philosophical minds is the highest, most perfect realization of the personal community. For us, on the contrary, that perfect realization is the kingdom of God, the Mystical Body, the communion of salvation offered us by God in Christ. Every earthly community of persons is only a reflection of that higher community and is moved interiorly by a natural desire for attaining the ultimate realization and fulfillment in the saving community of God's kingdom which is not of this world.

In conclusion we must recall once more how our pure view of those higher realities is endangered by inadequate symbolic images which, at the same time, we cannot avoid. We speak of a "body" and an "organism." Not only Christian theology but Hegel and Kant likewise use such images. When we hear that the whole person is a part of the community and is directed to the end of the community, we spontaneously think of the relation between the parts and the whole in an organism; and this image functions as a symbolic representation in our thinking. But organs are only functional parts of the whole in a natural organism, they have no meaning or value in themselves. The fulfillment of meaning is found only in the whole as such, and not in the parts. The whole is the end of the parts and not vice versa.

It was this fallacy that prompted some fascists and nazis to appeal to certain texts of St. Thomas to back up their total-

---

[5]Cf. especially the most careful analyses of François Grégoire in *Etudes Hégéliennes,* Louvain, 1958, pp. 31-39; 239-264.

itarian theories. By equating the personal community with a natural organism, they destroyed man's freedom and consequently also the personal community. Hence we must always keep in mind that the unity of the personal community, which we represent to ourselves in biological images, is at bottom totally different from the unity of a natural organism. The highest unity precisely includes and realizes the highest form of freedom. An image or symbol must never be allowed to obscure our view of the nature of a reality that cannot be properly represented but which we try to grasp by means of some image or symbol.

10. SOCIETY AND THE STATE

Another mistake committed by totalitarian theories, which likewise rests in part on a wrong interpretation of both Hegel and St. Thomas, consists in simply identifying society with a particular form of society, namely, with the state. First of all, the large portion of the human community that is circumscribed by the frontiers of a state is neither the only nor the most important unit in which man seeks to obtain a personal community. The family, the circle of friends, the religious community are in that respect much more important. Secondly, the state is not identical with the portion of mankind that is contained within its boundaries in virtue of sometimes accidental factors of race, language and history. The homogeneous or the heterogeneous community of people is the true reality which encompasses the many social phenomena and structures in its living density. To those structures belong both natural groups, such as families, spontaneous groups, such as a circle of friends, and associations for culture and recreation, for economic aims or other purposes.

Only in one particular respect, one particular relational connection, does the state coincide with the community of people. The state organizes the community of people into a public juridical community by enacting laws which determine the juridical order in a concrete way, and by creating forms of organization which regulate the application of those laws by means of constraint. Thus the state is a juridical community or society and as such is in clear contrast with the personal community. The latter is the ultimate earthly end of the state. The state serves the community of people by concretely developing, ordering and maintaining correct juridical relations that are directed to the realization of the person and hence of the personal community. The state has the function of a servant: it must foster and protect justice.

Rights, as we have seen, are based on the nature of the person. Man can have rights because he is a person. Personal right flows from the person's inviolable value and is traditionally referred to by the somewhat unsuitable term "natural law." However, personal right has to be worked out in the concrete and protected by the state, according to the demands of the historical situation and the possibilities of progress. It is the duty of the state to defend and protect the economic freedom and the moral freedom of the persons, of the citizens, against all unlawful violence. The state must give form and power to the demands of the sense of justice that is alive in the people. It must organize ownership, that is, the guaranteed right to have at one's disposal the material goods that are necessary for a good and free life, according to the demands of the inalienable personal rights of all men and the possibilities of the moment. The state must foster the national welfare and see that the available benefits are distributed to all persons and groups according to the demands of a proportional equality. It must call into existence the means and institutions necessary for the education, formation and culture of its citizens according to the capacities of the national income; and furthermore it must see that those facilities are at the disposal of everyone according to his personal need and ability. Thus the state has a serving and organizing function for the sake of realizing rights according to the people's sense of justice and the possibilities of its historical development.

11. THE JURIDICAL ORDER

The legal order is a complex order in which various juridical relations, some static, others more dynamic, are interwoven. First of all, there is the juridical relation covering individual persons and groups. To every person or group must be permitted or given what is due to them according to the definite rules of law and custom that express the sense of justice of the community.

Just conduct within the juridical order is called *commutative justice* after one of its principal activities. The object of this commutative justice is in itself somewhat abstract. It is reduced to purely businesslike relations of value between thing and thing and is calculated in a mechanical way, although in reality it contains elements that are not purely businesslike. For example, man's labor, for which he receives wages, does not simply belong to the order of things; but we reduce it to that order through an abstract consideration. Hence that juridical relation is in itself rather static.

That is why the exercise of commutative justice presupposes a more concrete and personalistic order in which the rules governing commutative justice are defined and adjusted to the demands of the rights of the person. The goods that are at the disposal of a community are limited. What is due to each person in his situation according to his needs, work, value and merit must be determined on the basis of the available whole and according to the demands of proportional personal equality. It belongs to *distributive justice* to determine what is just in that respect. Hence distributive justice is a dynamic factor in the determination of what in justice is due to each person or group of persons. Distributive justice requires constant revision. It is intimately connected with commutative justice, for it is a work of constantly readjusting the rules of the latter as demanded by the rights of the person and the possibilities of economic development.

In addition to the justice which regulates what is due to each person or group within the society of the state, there is a kind of justice that regulates what each person or group must contribute to the general welfare of the state. This justice also has a static aspect. Every citizen or group must contribute to the general welfare according to the state's laws. This constitutes *legal justice*. But this justice likewise demands constant correction and adjustment according to the development of society and the demands of proportional equality. The concrete elaboration of the implications in the dynamic task of legal justice is the function of what today is called *social justice*. Hence legal and social justice are intimately connected.

Finally, it is also evident that the right regulation of what is due to each person or group within the state is organically connected with the right regulation of what each person or group must contribute to the society of the state. For, it is impossible to give to everyone what is his due according to the rule of proportional equality if the contribution of each to the general good is not justly regulated according to the demands of proportional equality.

Accordingly, the whole order of justice constitutes a complex and very sensitive organic unity. The various orders of justice do not have their own closed domain. They permeate one another so deeply that general welfare can be realized only in the total harmonious regulation of all the relations of justice constituting the order of the state.

12. JUSTICE AND LOVE

We see then that the state is the overall organization of the public order of right and justice. The human person is, in a particular respect, a biological individual and as such has an inalienable right to dispose of the material goods needed for his life. In this, he is dependent on others and therefore he naturally forms with them an economic community. He is also a moral project for himself and as such has an inalienable right to education and to the objective goods that serve that purpose. In this, too, he is dependent on others and hence, by nature, forms with them a community of culture.

The two are *one* and are ordered to each other. The economic community that fosters the material freedom of personal existence is directed to the cultural community which helps to foster personal development and the moral freedom of the person. The state is the overall organization of law and justice, i.e., of the concrete public order of the cultural community in its economic incarnation. As such, its nature is sharply defined in contrast with the true personal community, to which it is nevertheless directed as to its ultimate end, viz., the fulfillment of the meaning of human existence.

The state is by its very nature incapable of entering into this higher order of the personal community and may not try to do so. The state is the domain of power. Its activity is the exercise of power. The personal community, which represents the value of an absolute end, is the domain of love and freedom. In this domain all force and power are meaningless. The world of personal self-realization, directed to the intersubjective communion of persons, determines the boundaries which the activity of political power is forbidden to transgress. The will to interfere by force in the world of inner conviction, where man recognizes what is true and good in his inner conscience, is the capital sin of the state.

In those matters the state has only the function of a servant. It must develop the means and the institutions that are needed by the citizens to educate themselves and their children according to the ideals that live in their hearts and their consciences; and it must put those means and institutions at their disposal according to the demands of proportional equality. The state must also defend the freedom of the citizens and groups in their striving for personal self-realization against all unjust attacks by others. It is to this that its task and power are confined.

Thus the domain of the state is the domain of justice and power within the total reality of the human community. The intersubjective community of persons, however, is the domain of love and freedom. With this conclusion we have reached the point where we shall be able to form a clear judgment

141

concerning the difference between justice and love and their mutual relations. But, in order to do so, we must first return to a fundamental idea which we have developed in the preceding chapter.

In my original experience of another person, he presents himself to me as another free and independent subject in his inviolable character of being "someone else" and of "being other than I." The moral claim which the other person makes upon my conscience, that is, my moral freedom, is twofold. It is, first of all, a claim to respect. I must leave and give to him what he needs for his bodily existence and welfare, as well as for his personal self-formation. To order my conduct according to that claim is to be just. Secondly, that claim is permeated with an invitation that goes deeper; an invitation to serve his objective good disinterestedly and actively and thus to form with him a communion of inter-subjectivity in which I achieve my own personality, thus earning my own most profound happiness. To respond to that invitation is to love.

At once I can see now that justice and love are one in their deepest nature. This unity is established by love. The moral attitude toward the other is an objective, disinterested affirmation of his person for himself, and this attitude is love. To this objective affirmation belongs, above all, that I respect the boundary established by his personal inviolability. To respect this boundary is precisely to leave and give to him what is due to him. Justice then is a first and, as it were, minimum requirement and condition of love. I first consent to the other in his otherness and then direct myself to the core of his personal being with a will of disinterested and generous service; and there I find myself in him as in my own self. Hence there is certainly no love without justice, since justice is the minimum demand and the condition of love. If I am not just, I certainly cannot truly love. On the other hand, there is no true justice without love. If I am selfish or proud, I will also not be just by inner conviction. I will then be just only under pressure and because I am afraid of force.

This defect of love gives rise to the state. If the community of persons were realized in a pure and universal way, justice would be a natural and normal act of love, and hence of freedom. But pure love is a very rare phenomenon in our sinful world—so rare that it makes us think of heaven. For this reason the order of justice becomes an independent order under the control of the state. It is true, therefore, that the state, in its essential power to use force, is the result of sin and human imperfection. Hence a profound truth is contained in the strong words which Ortega y Gasset wrote: "While society is the inevitable condition on which man can be man, it is at the same time his true hell."[6] Nearly all utopias bear witness to the fact that man really feels that way. Their testimony betrays a certain understanding of the fact that the personal community in the sphere of absolute freedom is the object of our most profound desires. The communist utopia, too, which thinks of an earthly final kingdom in which the state will no longer have any function because all men will be good, is inspired by the same idea. We have lost paradise and the state has come in its place until we can find paradise again. But this will not happen on earth but in heaven.

From this view follows with perfect logic the great socio-ethical principle which we shall develop in the next chapter and which reads: "As much freedom as possible, and as much compelling force as is necessary." The exercise of force is a necessary evil. Auguste Comte, who favored an authoritarian organization of the state, saw already that the exercise of power leads to "radical degradation."[7] That is why we must be grateful to those men who for noble motives are willing to devote themselves to the necessary but ungrateful work of government that brings with it such great dangers for their own personality.

---

[6] Ortega y Gasset, *Del imperio romano, Obras,* VI, quinta edicion, Madrid, 1961, p. 72.
[7] *Ibid,* p. 114.

13. THE COMMON GOOD

These explanations permit us now to define clearly what is meant by the *bonum commune,* the common good of society. This common good too must be considered on two different levels. Looked at metaphysically, it is the all-embracing well-being of all persons in the community of love. That God is the common good of the universe can be fully clarified only in Christian terms. God is love. Creation is the expression of His love. This means that nature was created for finite persons, and these are called into existence by God in order that they may acquire personal fulfillment of being in a loving community with Himself and with the other created persons. This is salvation. The realization of the personal community through love is the *bonum divinum,* the divine good, and in it lies God's glory: the manifestation of His most profound being which is love. The philosopher cannot penetrate into that, because it belongs to the order of grace. But the Christian philosopher, encouraged by that model presented by faith and reasoning from his own principles, can and must establish that the personal community in freedom and love is the ultimate common good of human society, the ultimate end of all striving for unity, and the fulfillment of the intention of creation.

When we consider it on that ideal level, there is no opposition between the common good and the private good. For, as we have said, on that level, the realization of the community coincides with the realization of the person. The two are identical. On this level every opposition between private good and common good would be a contradiction and would encroach upon the good of the individual as well as upon that of the community.

On the level of the juridical society, ordered by the state in an all-embracing manner, the common good is "general welfare." This general welfare is the best possible realization of justice in all its relations. For, as we have seen, the various domains of justice form an organic unity within which the good order of the one depends on the good order of the other. On this level there appears an opposition and tension between the common good of the community and the private good of the individual. This tension can be solved only in an unstable and ever-to-be reconstructed harmony, by the proper exercise of distributive and social justice under the guidance of the state.

It stands to reason that the general welfare is directed to the divine common good of the community of persons. In this ultimate end-value the two find once more their original unity, but only in such a way that their distinction in the existing earthly order can never be overcome. To dream that the ideal will some day be fulfilled in this world is to live in utopia.

CHAPTER SEVEN

SOCIO-ETHICAL PRINCIPLES

1. CHARACTER AND RANGE OF SOCIO-ETHICAL PRINCIPLES

In Chapter Two we have briefly analyzed the various phases of thought concerning society and, defining our own plan, confined ourselves to the general doctrine concerning society. This doctrine comprises two phases. The first determines and analyzes the ethical nature of man as the person who makes society and the ethical nature of the earthly community of persons that results from it. This task we have tried to complete in the two preceding chapters. Still to be explained is the second phase which is concerned with the general principles that express and unfold our understanding of the ethical nature proper to the human community. This we shall try to do in the present chapter.

Just as our mental grasp of being is made explicit and expressed in a number of general metaphysical principles, so also we must unfold our mental grasp of man's ethico-social reality in a number of general socio-ethical principles.

The fundamental social principles we shall now discuss are most general. They follow from the essence of the human community and are applicable to every community in which man as man, that is, as a personal whole, is involved. A certain distinction is presupposed here between communities in which man as a person is connected with his fellow-men and, on the other hand, various associations and organizations in which he freely binds himself to others in one respect or another for a variety of practical purposes. The associations are formed within the general human community and, on that account, are within the domain where our principles find legitimate application. This applicability, however, is not based on their own special nature but on the fact that they are structures of the general human community. It is clear, for example, that a financial association must practice tolerance with respect to its members, not because it is a financial association, but because it is inserted into the larger human community. The problem of tolerance is, strictly speaking, meaningless within a financial society as such. Hence the application of the principle of tolerance does not acquire in that case a special inner modality as a consequence of the nature of the association.

On the contrary, in the family, the nation, the Church or in mankind, and also in a club of friends or a religious community, man is involved as a person, that is, with his whole being. The general moral imperatives address themselves to man as a member of those groups. For this reason we must take into account that these groups realize the idea of community in a manner that is intrinsically diverse and that, as a consequence, the principles as applied within the various forms of such groups acquire diverse modalities. Tolerance in a monastery, for example, cannot go as far as to permit one of its members to hold atheistic views. For the religious conviction of theism is the very foundation of such a community.

The general socio-ethical principles express in human judgments our ideas about the ethical nature of the human community. This community means here the community of the integral man who by means of his body pursues his spiritual being in a material world. It does not mean a community of souls but a community of men. That is why it is necessary for us to look at the structured whole of the human community as essentially unified. This community is an organized cultural community, incarnate in an economic structure and directed to a loving community of persons.

Culture, incarnate in the community's body, is a realm of means[1] directed to the absolute end, viz., the loving com-

---

[1]The terms "means" and "end" are as inadequate to express the relation of the economic community and cultural community to the community of persons as they are to explain the relation between body and soul. For want of better terms we use the terms "means" and "end" but give them the following sense. "Means" does not refer to something that exhausts its significance by helping us attain something else in which the means is not preserved. Only in and by what, for want of a better term, we here call "means" can the end

munity of persons. The common good of that community is the total good of the persons in the personal community. The general welfare, or the just ordering of the economic goods and the objective cultural values, belong also to the common good as an order of means that are indispensable to the personal community which is to be realized in and by man's earthly bodily being. All this we have fully analyzed in the preceding chapters. This we must keep carefully in mind in order to realize that the general socio-ethical principles are nothing but judgments expressing our ethical view of the incarnated community of persons in the form of general imperatives.

For, as socio-ethical imperatives, they would have no place in a pure personal community considered in the abstract and free from an economic incarnation in a cultural community. Of course, incarnation is required in order that a community of persons be able to exist as something human. Whenever there exists any form of social life in a world of culture, our socio-ethical principles come into force because of the community of persons with its absolute value and obligatory character. For this reason the imperative of love itself is not a socio-ethical principle. Love is the all-embracing fundamental ethical attitude of persons toward other persons. It is the ultimate ethical absolute, and every authentic moral imperative is implicitly contained in it. Socio-ethical imperatives are specific ethical imperatives that express and translate the demands of love with respect to the social domain. The fundamental attitude of love expresses itself in a multitude of activities which man exercises by his body in a world of nature and culture that is pre-given as his social environment.

---

be attained. Hence the realization of the means belongs as an integral factor to the achievement of the end. Within that final fulfillment the means continues to exist in a subordinate way; and what we call "means" obtains its final value and meaning only in the realization of what we call an "end." Hence the "means" in our present use of the term has not merely a passing value but a permanent means-value that is wholly directed to that final achievement as the giver of meaning. This final end represents an absolute value without which the rest would have no definite value at all.

Those activities take on specific forms and lead to structures by which man is taken up into many kinds of social units. The whole of those structures constitutes the social domain. Socio-ethical principles are principles that regulate the relations between different groups or between persons and groups. It is possible, and *a priori* probable, that those principles, in their most general form, have a wider field of application than that of the strictly social domain. They are only socio-ethical insofar as they are applied to the social realm and can thus be formulated with a particular modality. Socio-ethical principles are general ethical imperatives to be obeyed in the formation and development of the social groups as well as in the conduct of those groups toward one another or in relation to the members and, conversely also, in the conduct of the members toward the groups. They must be obeyed because they are ultimately directed to the absolute core of the common good, the loving community of persons.

We shall not enter into the discussion regarding the number of socio-ethical principles that can be distinguished. We accept three. Love demands that we serve the integral personal good of the others in a disinterested way. It is in this that its proper act consists. In man's concrete earthly existence, this service leads to the formation of social structures that are directed to mutual assistance. The ethical imperative that prompts the formation of such groups is the principle of solidarity. But love requires also, and precisely because of the end-value of the other's personal good, that we respect his freedom and responsibility as much as possible, not only in the exercise of group activities but also in the person's life and expression of his most intimate convictions. To this requirement correspond two ethical imperatives, which not infrequently go somewhat together, namely, the principle of subsidiarity and the principle of tolerance.

2. The Principle of Solidarity

Much could be said about the term and concept of "solidarity." The word is derived from the Latin juridical term *"in solidum,"* which means that each of the persons in a group is responsible not only in part but for the whole. The word later was used in a wider and more general sense to signify various ways of mutual dependence or belonging together.

As early as 1707 Adam Ferguson, in his *Essay on the History of Civil Society,* pointed out that the differential division of labor gives rise to a solidarity between those who are involved in a single process of work according to various skills and functions. The term was later adopted in descriptive sociology to signify the various structures from which active unity of purpose arises. Thus E. Durkheim, in his *De la division du travail* (1893), made a distinction between mechanical solidarity (*solidarité méchanique*) based on unity in similarity and organic solidarity (*solidarité organique*) based on unity in diversity. From this, Durkheim even developed a sociological typology. According to him, the structure of primitive communities is characterized principally by mechanical solidarity but, in more developed societies, on account of the differential division of labor and collaboration in diversity, organic solidarity predominates. This solidarity, he says, should create a community structure in which the individual is no longer directly connected with the whole but only indirectly, by means of more specialized associations. These associations are based on intrinsically differentiated complexes of work and life.

It is easy to understand that the term solidarity would not continue to signify only the objective belonging-together that is based on objective structures of life, but was quite naturally applied also to the subjective solidarity that flows from that objective solidarity and is experienced in feeling and action. Only a short step further was necessary to arrive at the ethical notion of solidarity in the sense of an obligation to "togetherness." As early as 1840, Pierre Leroux attached that ethical meaning to the term *"solidarité"* when he wrote in *De l'Humanité* that it is an obligation of mutual assistance, based on the idea that the community of which one is a member forms a whole. In France this idea led to the formation of a social doctrine of solidarity that became the myth, as it were, of the Third Republic, until World War I. The principal proponent of that doctrine was L. Bourgeois. He looked upon the whole of civilization as a gift made by the preceding generations; the new generations were taken up in it as beneficiaries prior to any exercise of their own individual role; they had therefore the obligation, spelled out in detail by laws, to accept and work for the further development of the goods they had inherited from the past.

This positivistic solidarism proved incapable of maintaining itself amidst the trials of World War I. Between the two world wars a social doctrine called "solidarism" was developed in the Catholic world; its principal theorists were H. Pesch and G. Grundlach. They started from the idea that man's existence is by its very nature social and that society, likewise, can exist only in and by men who live and act in a conscious way. Hence man, considered ontologically and in virtue of his concrete nature, is totally directed to the community, but conversely, the whole community is also directed to living men. The good of every individual is ultimately the good of the whole community, but the good of the community is also inclusively the good of all the individuals. This ontological solidarity, following from man's nature, expresses also an essential characteristic of man's life in a community. This the French positivists were said to have shown very well. Because society is constructed by the will of man under the guidance of reason, the principle of solidarity is at the same time an ethical principle; and considered in the material reality of earthly existence, it is a juridical principle that must guide the development and ordering of the social structures.

Because of certain historical connotations, the term "solidarism" has lost much of its popularity since World War II. "Personalism" is now the preferred expression. Both views follow the same general line of thought, but they do not coincide perfectly, at least in the sense that personalism was

151

born from a deeper insight into the ethical nature of man and presents a more developed form of pre-war solidarism. Hence there is a significant difference in the terms "personalism" and "solidarism." Personalism does not base society on ontological solidarity as on its fundamental principle, but on the nature of man as man, that is, as a person who is for himself an ethical task, a vocation which he must realize himself as a person by living for others. Man as man is an ethical being, determined by the vocation of love. For this reason the individual person's orientation to the loving community of persons constitutes the fundamental principle of the personalistic theory of society.

Accordingly, E. Welty was not entirely wrong when he criticized solidarism because it made too great a separation between a primary order of being and a subsequent order of purpose: "The order of being and the order of purpose must be understood in terms of one another, for they constitute one order. . . . Individual man and community have no mutually dependent existence; neither can they be understood independently of each other."[2] In our opinion the idea of solidarity can be conceived in a clear and pure way only if we do not start from an ontological situation but from the ethical character of the person. Undoubtedly, a most important principle is expressed in the statement that man, prior to any conscious act, already finds himself in society and can exist only in and through it, just as society is a reality only in and through him. We have repeatedly stressed this principle in the preceding pages.

However, that solidarity is not the ultimate foundation of social ethics. This foundation lies in the ethical nature of the person who can realize and fulfill himself as a person only in a total activity that is disinterestedly directed to the

---

[2] E. Welty, *Gemeinschaft und Einzelmensch,* Salzburg, 1935, p. 384: "Seinhafte und zielhafte Ordnung müssen auseinander verstanden werden; denn sie bilden eine einzige Ordnung . . . Einzelmensch und Gemeinschaft haben kein voneinander unabhängiges Dasein; sie können auch nicht unabhängig begriffen werden."

good of others. What comes first in the order of understanding is not existence through the community, but existence for the community. The ultimate basic explanation is not given by ontological "togetherness" but by "togetherness" in the metaphysico-ethical sense. We say "in the metaphysico-ethical sense" because man's ethical destiny for the loving community expresses most profoundly the metaphysical nature of man, the mystery of the person.

Thus the fundamental principle of personalism offers the ultimate basis for the justification of the socio-ethical principle of solidarity. Solidarity is the ethical bond that unites men in a social task: in the very exercise of his part-function, every member, as a rational and moral being, consciously accepts care and reponsibility for the whole. He experiences his task as a contribution to the whole and, therefore, in its exercise he adjusts himself entirely to the demands of the whole.

This meaning shows a pure semantic development from the original meaning of *"in solidum."* In solidarity we, together, face the common task. We stand side by side. Our attention is fixed on the execution of a plan in which we are involved together. It is in this that solidarity is different from love. In love we face one another. Our attention is fixed on the total personal good of the other.

The principle of solidarity states that when the individual faces a necessary task which he cannot properly accomplish by himself, he may count upon the orderly help of others for the fulfillment of that task. In other words, when a fellow-man faces a task which is necessary or useful for his personal well-being, but which he is unable to accomplish alone, we are obliged to help him to the best of our possibilities. The first formula starts from the person's need of assistance. It is an "I-formula": "I need you, hence it is my right." The second formula starts from a person's obligation to help. It is a "you-formula": "You need me, hence it is my duty." These formulae complete each other. They merge in a "we-formula": "Where we, that is, all men on earth, are faced with a task which no one man is able to achieve alone, we are solidarily (*in solidum*) obliged to assist one another to accomplish that task in a common effort."

In the concrete situation of life on earth, this solidarity means, on the part of the community, an obligation to foster or create, within its historical possibilities, all organizations and undertakings that are necessary or useful to supply the members with the material and spiritual goods required for the satisfaction of their individual wants and the fulfillment of their personal vocation. As we have explained in detail in the preceding chapter, it is impossible for man to satisfy his biological needs and achieve his personal culture if he is left to himself. He needs the help of others. The principle of solidarity is socio-ethical insofar as the obligation to form proper social organs for the mutual assistance of the community and all its members weighs upon the members *"in solidum."* But insofar as it regulates the exercise of the dynamic function of justice by responsible authorities, it is a general and supreme juridical principle. The principle of solidarity is the guiding socio-ethical norm of social justice, as we have explained above.

The ultimate foundation of the principle of solidarity is the ethical nature of man which, as we have said in our central thesis, means that man can attain the perfection of his manhood only in being for others. The attitude of love demands that we disinterestedly serve the personal good of the other and, hence, that we apply ourselves to fulfill all the conditions that are necessary for the attainment of that personal good. In our earthly community the union of persons can be pursued only through our bodily existence in a cultural community. This implies that all are solidarily responsible for the creation of the social structures which can best serve to satisfy the material wants of the individual and the cultural needs of the person in his self-formation. Thus the principle of solidarity is directly aimed at the realization of the general welfare, the best possible order of justice, which in turn is ultimately directed to the common good of the community of persons—loving unity of persons.

3. THE PRINCIPLE OF SUBSIDIARITY

The principle of subsidiarity intrinsically complements the principle of solidarity. The principle of solidarity is the dynamic principle governing the creation and development of social structures. It gives concrete expression to the spirit of the saying "One for all and all for one." The principle of subsidiarity adds a certain reservation, a certain condition, which also flows immediately from the ethical nature of man, namely, that one must allow the community to construct and develop itself with the greatest possible freedom. This principle presupposes that the universal community has an essentially organic structure, that the persons are at first in community with one another in smaller groups, especially the family, but afterwards are taken up, in various ways, into larger communities, which ultimately integrate into the universal community. The principle of subsidiarity maintains then that, in the process of constructing an organic community, both the smaller particular groups and the individual persons must be accorded as much freedom as is permitted by the general welfare.

Thus we see that the principle of subsidiarity is the principle of social freedom of movement. As a general principle that applies to all earthly societies, including the family, it is a socio-ethical principle. Insofar as it binds the authorities in their efforts to realize a just legal order, it is a general juridical principle that is sometimes formulated in slogans such as: "As much freedom as possible, as much constraint as is necessary." The principle of subsidiarity must inspire especially the exercise of distributive justice in the sense we have defined above.

In Catholic socio-ethical doctrine, the idea of subsidiarity has been raised to the rank of the leading social principle, especially under the influence of Pius XI's *Quadragesimo Anno*. In this encyclical the pope deplored that the invidualistic spirit has led to the destruction of the rich, natural texture of associations that existed between the individual and state organization. On that occasion he formulated the

the *"subsidiarii" officii principium,* i.e., the principle according to which the state must fulfill a "subsidiary" function with respect to the family and organically developed social life. According to the Latin meaning of that term, it is a function similar to that of reserve troops in time of war; in other words it has to come to the rescue, help out where regular troops are inadequate. "Just as it is wrong to withdraw from the individual and commit to the community at large what private enterprise and industry can accomplish, so too, it is an injustice, a grave evil and a disturbance of right order for a larger and higher organization to arrogate to itself functions which can be performed efficiently by smaller and lower bodies. This is a fundamental principle of social philosophy, unshaken and unchangeable, and it retains its full truth today. Of its very nature the true aim of all social activity should be to help individual members of the social body, but never to destroy or absorb them."[3]

This principle presupposes in the first place the theory we have developed in Chapter Six, according to which it is necessary to make a clear distinction between the living community that maintains a definite bond with the state, and the state itself. The latter by means of power—that is, legislation, command and sanction—constructs, protects and maintains a legal order of justice in a measure which is beyond the community's free development. The absolute ideal, as the Marxists clearly realized, is a completely free community in which the state has no longer any function. But the realization of this ideal is not of this world because of the antisocial tendencies that afflict mankind. In the historical situation of mankind, complete freedom would be identical with anarchy. The justly exercised use of force by the state is necessary to prevent unbridled and unjust violence of person against person and group against group, "the war of all against all" (*bellum omnium contra omnes*).

---

[3]Pius XI, *Quadragesimo Anno,* A. A. S., vol. XXIII (1931), p. 203; *On the Reconstruction of the Social Order* (translation) America Press, 1938, New York, p. 23.

In this sense the exercise of force by the state is necessary to protect the freedom of persons and groups against violent and unjust aggression. The state is also indispensable for fostering the construction of community life according to the demands of solidarity. To protect freedom and to foster the projects and tasks of solidarity or to help in the realization of those tasks: these are the twofold functions of the state. This Pius XI had already clearly expressed in his encyclical on Christian education: "The function therefore of the civil authority residing in the state is twofold: to protect and to foster, but by no means to absorb the family and the individual, or to substitute itself for them."[4]

The capital sin of the state is always that of simply identifying itself with the human community and thus claiming that it is the ultimate end within this world. The state then tries to realize itself perfectly according to the logic of its own means. It then claims to have the task of regulating everything by means of legislation, orders and force. This leads logically to the desire to regulate the whole man, his whole life, even his thoughts and feelings, and fix them in a state-imposed mold. But a system of law and force that lays claim to the whole man in every respect is precisely the idea of the totalitarian state. Just as a kingdom of absolute freedom in complete, unforced harmony would be the realization of heaven upon earth, so a successful totalitarian state which has the whole man in its power would be the best image of hell upon earth. Such a state would not only be the "anti-christ" but also the "antiman."

For this reason it is necessary to make a sharp distinction between the living community and the state, and to cling to the principle that the state has, with respect to the human community which it contains, the function of a servant. The state must protect and defend freedom and always foster it. For, to the extent that the state helps the community to

---

[4]*Divini Illius Magistri,* A. A. S., vol. XXII (1930), p. 63; translation, *Christian Education of Youth,* Paulist Press, N. Y., p. 16.

develop the institutions and structures that enable men to win material and moral freedom according to the demands of solidarity, to that same extent the state also takes away the reasons that make its intervention necessary. In the measure in which it is successful in this task, the state eliminates itself as an apparatus of power and lightens its coercive and repressive functions. In this sense good politics is an education to freedom.

Thus the use of force and coercion is to the historical life of mankind what asceticism is in regard to individual human history. Man, as he actually is, cannot achieve the moral freedom of virtue without imposing a certain restraint on the spontaneous urgings of his nature and without constant watchfulness. So also mankind cannot rise to an ever greater social and civil freedom without a wise control of the anti-social tendencies in the body of the community and without constant watchfulness on the part of the government. But just as asceticism becomes less burdensome to the extent that virtue or moral freedom are developed in the individual person, so will the hand of the state weigh less and less heavily upon the people as the spirit of moral freedom grows in the living community. To view the exercise of civil authority as the self-asceticism of mankind on its way to an ever greater freedom is undoubtedly a beautiful idea.

The principle of subsidiarity is indeed the great principle of social education. Education is by its very nature the opposite of putting oneself in the place of the pupil and dictating to him his personal decisions. To educate means to assist another in forming his own correct judgment, and in making wise decisions for his own life. To educate is to help another in self-education, and the latter can ultimately come only from the freedom and the responsibility of the one who is being educated. If we wish to educate someone to freedom, we must also give him as much freedom of movement and initiative as possible and use coercion only when it happens to be necessary. That is why Friedrich

Schiller says the following about the aesthetic state: "To give freedom is the fundamental law of this kingdom."[5]

The basic pedagogical principle, then, is that the educator must endeavor to advance his pupil to the point where he lives so excellently by his own rational freedom that the educator's intervention is finally unnecessary. This pedagogical principle is broadened into the principle of subsidiarity and made into a socio-ethical principle. The principle is now applied not only to the relations of person to person but also to the relation of group to person and of larger groups to smaller groups: do not absorb or replace, but foster free unfolding and development, and intervene only to the extent that the common good of the all-embracing community demands it.

This common good, as we know already, is ultimately the personal good of all as far as it is to be fulfilled here on earth in and by the social groups in which the person is taken up. The end of society, and hence also of every form of common life, is the growth of its members in personality. That is why it has as its task to help the members, according to its own nature and with its own means, to attain that degree of material freedom and of moral freedom which makes them free for the union of persons, the community of love, which is the ultimate end and the supreme common good of the community in all its members and on every level.

Freedom that creates the proper climate of love and of perfect communion is an aspect of the absolute good. The intervention of the higher in the lower, which limits the freedom of a person or of an association of persons can be justified only on the basis of the demands of freedom itself. When, because of mankind's immoral tendencies, the free play of liberty is directed against the development of free life by its repression of the others' freedom or by sloth, disunity and disorder, then a superior power must

---

[5]"Freiheit zu schenken durch Freiheit ist das Grundgesetz dieses Reichs." *Über die ästhetische Erziehung des Menschen*, Brief 27, *Werke*, Stuttgart, 1955, Vol. V, p. 372.

intervene in the name of freedom itself in order to protect and foster it. Thus it follows that the principle of subsidiarity has absolute and universal validity in the realm of the person: as much freedom as is permitted by the common good, and only as much coercion as is demanded by the common good, which, ultimately, is but the good of freedom itself. This principle is universally valid. In the first place, it applies to the state with respect to all groups and persons that live within its territory. It is also applicable to every community within the state in relation to partial groups and persons that are organic parts of the larger community.

We are now able to formulate the principle of subsidiarity with full clarity and to explain its relation to the principle of solidarity. It will perhaps be best to use once more the analogy of education, for the principles regarding the person are analogous to one another on every level we may wish to consider.

Above all, the educator places himself disinterestedly at the service of his pupil's personality development. With a disinterested desire to serve, he becomes solidary with his pupil in the latter's task of self-formation, which the pupil certainly cannot achieve by himself. For this reason he puts at the disposal of his pupil all the means that are necessary for that self-formation. He helps him by word and action; but he would be going counter to his own intentions if he were to do for his pupil what can be useful and formative for the latter only if he does it in free self-activity.

We find something similar in the relation between the community and the person. Above all the community— which means here "all *in solidum*"—has the task to construct and develop a community, a socially structured whole, so that it becomes for the persons an efficient organization of assistance to satisfy their individual needs and to learn as well as possible their "profession of being man" (*métier d'homme*). This is the principle of solidarity. In the construction of the community, however, the relationship of the groups to the members, and of the higher and larger groups to the lower and more restricted groups, must be conceived in such a way that the former help the latter in the fulfillment of their task. This is the positive aspect of the principle of subsidiarity. The help must be given in such a way that the others are aided precisely in developing themselves by free self-activity within the larger group; and they are subject to coercion only when, and to the extent that, they are acting contrary to the common good of the higher community. This is the negative aspect of the principle of subsidiarity.

The ultimate ethical idea that justifies the principle of subsidiarity is the same as that which forms the basis of the principle of solidarity. It is the imperative that makes man a man and defines his ethical nature. This imperative reads: "Let there be a community of persons," which is the same as saying: "Let personality be." For the "act" that constitutes the personality as a perfect personality is love, which is also the "act" that constitutes the community of persons. Love disinterestedly wills the good of the other and finds objective joy in the realization of this good. But the good that is willed by the lover and in which he experiences unselfish joy, is the personal good of the other, the realization and fulfillment of the latter's personal value. Now this is a value which the loved one cannot receive passively from the lover, but which he must realize actively from and through himself. The good of the person is a good that, by definition, can be acquired only by the person's freedom. For this reason the method of love in the service of the other is one of assistance and invitation. It makes the lover supply to the other the means that enable him to realize himself. It appeals to his freedom, prompting him to tend to the goal by self-activity. Love, then, respects, demands and fosters the other's freedom.

Accordingly, the ethical imperative of love, worked out intelligently in the social reality of our earthly existence, unfolds in two ways. On the one hand, it becomes the principle of solidarity, the socio-ethical obligation of developing the auxiliary organs required by the community to the extent that they are technically possible. On the other hand, it leads to the principle of subsidiarity, the socio-ethical demand that within the organization of society the broader and higher groups complement the world of the smaller and lower groups, without going beyond this subsidiary role.

The principle of subsidiarity must always be applied with intelligence and good judgment especially in politics. It must not be permitted to degenerate into a reactionary principle which would try to justify the retention of the *status quo* when historical development has progressed beyond it. Such an artificial conservatism would be harmful to the general welfare. The principle of subsidiarity becomes such a one-sided and reactionary conservative principle when it is interpreted in the ideological context of a static, anti-historical concept of the community. Human society is not a static replica of an eternal order, but it is a dynamic, historical enterprise directed to an ideal order. The historical development of the community constantly remolds the living matter of humanity and pours it forever into new and unpredictable forms. It is the duty of the state to assist the birth and growth of that which is adapted to the new phase of history. This duty implies also that the state must encourage the disappearance of structures that are antiquated and unadaptable but to which certain groups continue to cling for selfish motives or through lack of understanding. Common welfare and freedom require the state to act in this way, for unimpeded progress toward a fuller realization of freedom belongs to the essence of general welfare.

Sound politics that understands its "subsidiary" role realizes that the free and spontaneous initiative of the citizens must be respected, encouraged and supported when they try to realize more appropriately adjusted structures of life and institutions. It must try to provide room and possibilities for that free initiative, without which man suffocates and becomes petrified in passively served organizations.

The state must intervene in lower associations and take over their tasks only when the necessary initiative is wanting in them or when they are incapable of executing the necessary projects. It must impede and restrain private initiatives only when and to the extent that these work against the general welfare of the free ethical community.

What concretely corresponds to the demands of subsidiarity in each particular historical situation, must be determined in each case by what we have designated in our general plan as the "third phase" of reflection upon the community. In every case, however, it should be evident that the civil authorities, according to the situations, should allow more freedom at one time and less at another. There occur periods of crisis in the history of a people or a culture in which an almost dictatorial system is practically indispensable for the preservation of society. This is then the only possible solution but, of course, it satisfies no one and is accepted only because there is no other way. In such cases, the politician must not forget that, to use a metaphor, even the severest winter will be followed by spring and that it would be wrong to pursue a political line which aims at perpetuating a severe regimentation. On the contrary, he must try to create conditions which will permit greater freedom. The fundamental problem here is always the moral situation and the moral education of the people. It is only with morally free persons that a free community of citizens can be constructed in an orderly way.

4. THE PRINCIPLE OF TOLERANCE

The principle of solidarity is the most general ethical principle that guides the development of community forms in which persons help one another in their biological and human formation and in which they live their personal community life as earthly human beings. The principles of subsidiarity affirms that in this project of solidarity, which extends to the whole organically constructed community, the various groups must help and complement their sub-groups and ultimately their members in their self-activity without absorbing or oppressing them. It is necessary to allow as much initiative and freedom to the persons in their individual and social development as are permitted by the demands of the general welfare.

Granting and respecting the other's freedom goes so far that the existence of divergent convictions about life, on the basis of which diverse groups or members plan and develop their existence in the world and in the community, does not *per se* cancel the demands of solidarity and subsidiarity. This point is affirmed by the principle of tolerance. In its most general formulation this third principle, like the first two, applies to a larger domain than the purely social realm. It regulates also the individual relations of man to man. As we saw above, in the pedagogical relation the educator exercises in an eminent way with respect to his pupil the general solidarity and subsidiarity to which love invites man in relation to his fellow-man. Tolerance is likewise primarily an attitude of person to person. It maintains solidarity and subsidiarity in earthly coexistence, even where profound differences in conviction and opinion separate human beings from one another.

Tolerance is an attitude of a person or group of persons toward another person or group insofar as these are "different." The "otherness" in question does not arise from natural differences, such as race or temperament, nor from unimportant differences in opinion, but is based on more profound differences of conviction concerning the ultimate questions of existence, concerning that which man ultimately accepts as the fundamental truth and value. From such a difference follows a different interpretation of existence, hence a divergent project of life that expresses itself in personal and social activities and conduct.

The ethical attitude which a person must take with respect to another person who differs from him in his view of the world and of life is called "tolerance." The term "tolerance" signifies a rather secondary aspect of the attitude in question.

It means that we let the other act freely in his being-different, not for opportunistic reasons, but on the fundamental ethical grounds that we respect the other's inviolable character as a person. Thus the primary aspect of that attitude is something positive, viz., to respect the freedom of the persons. The fact, however, that men adhere to different convictions and opinions in the most fundamental questions of life, is an evil. The ideal good would be the unity of all in the acknowledgment of the true and the real good. I cannot rejoice when I see that others do not share a conviction of life which I consider true and good. If I did rejoice I would not be convinced of my view. Thus I take upon myself a painful burden when I make the noble gesture of wholeheartedly letting my fellow-man be free to follow his own conviction.

Tolerance is not confined to letting the other adhere interiorly to a different conviction. It also leaves him free to live according to that conviction, that is, to express it in word and conduct and to form social organizations with those who share the same opinions. For man is *one,* his life is an interiority that expresses itself in outward behavior. The latter is the outer side, so to speak, of the former; and, because man is an incarnate spirit in the world, the outer side is indissolubly connected with his interiority. It would be pharisaical and insincere if we wished to limit tolerance to interior convictions only.

Tolerance means to let another act freely. Negatively it means that we abstain from any kind of coercion, physical or moral, by which we might make one who thinks differently change his conviction or prevent him, as existing in this world, from following his own way of life.

The ultimate ethical foundation of tolerance is love. The person is by definition a being who owns his life as something proper to him, as something of himself. By the fact that God created him, he has received his life in his own keeping. He himself is responsible for it. As a person, he can lead his own self-responsible life only from and by his own innerly guided freedom, that is, as guided by his conscience. Conscience, by its very definition, is strictly personal, untouchable and inviolable. Conscience can guide man's life only in the light of convictions which man adheres to with personal conviction. Any other kind of life is unreal, untrue, and hence unworthy of the person. Now love puts itself at the service of the total personal good of the other, and this personal good is by definition a good that the other can recognize and strive for only in full freedom. As a consequence, respect for the other's freedom is an intrinsic condition that must of necessity be present in every loving orientation to the other.

A Christian receives particular enlightenment about this matter from his faith. God has revealed Himself to the Christian as love. In His method of salvation through the prophets and Christ, He has given the most pure example of tolerance. Respect for freedom belongs essentially to God's method of vocation. When the God of love calls, He shows the utmost respect for human freedom. He permits even the possibility that man will opt for the decisive and eternal rejection of God that is essentially included in his God-given freedom.

At the same time, it follows that tolerance does not exclude the apostolic zeal of an active invitation. On the contrary, in a man of conviction tolerance is an inner condition that accompanies his inviting attitude. Tolerance and zeal are two mutually complementary attitudes which love imposes on the strongly convinced mind in man's dealings with those who think otherwise. Because I desire the other's personal good, I desire also that he may participate in the truth and the value which so convincingly animate my conscious life. I will for the other the true and highest personal good, and this includes the recognition of truth and authentic value. But precisely because it is personal, this good cannot be acquired by the other except in full freedom. That is why I fully respect his conscience and conviction. To this must be added that a man must look upon every attempt to force his conscience as an attack upon his being a person. He will naturally react to such an attack by antipathy for the person or group which has attacked him; and he will also be prompted to dislike the cause which they serve and the belief which leads them to act in that intolerant way.

This reaction is not only a fact of experience but a psychological law flowing from man's awareness of his personal value. Intolerance, then, goes counter to the very intention of love which desires to meet the other in a community of truth. Tolerance, on the contrary, does not act like a brake on the tendency of love, but is rather a condition that is favorable for its exercise. This additional reflection helps to show that love is the essential foundation of tolerance.

Accordingly, tolerance does not exclude zeal for one's own conviction, the apostolic, missionary spirit, or a militant defense of one's faith. The only thing which tolerance demands in those matters is that no means be used which are not in harmony with the respect we must have for the conscience and the inviolable dignity of our fellow-man.

We may also use this occasion to eliminate the prejudice that the believer, the man who is absolutely convinced that what he believes about the ultimate questions of life is true, is incapable of being tolerant. On the contrary, only in one who has a rock-fast conviction can tolerance reach perfect nobility and beauty. Conviction is the driving force of the mind. A firm but authentic conviction is the very best climate for mental health; uncertainty and doubt are a sickness of the mind. The lack of all conviction is equivalent to death. In order that one may be tolerant in the full sense of the word, he must realize on the basis of his own experience what it means to have a conviction and cherish it. Only then will he be able to realize what the other's conviction means to the one who thinks differently. Only then will he be fully aware of the value that he respects in the other by his tolerance.

It is true, of course, that believers through mistaken zeal have often been intolerant. However, it is no less true that the most chivalrous battles between men who thought differently, but discoursed with one another in mutual trust, respect and friendship, have given expression to some of the most sublime manifestations of magnanimity recorded in human history. The noblest paragon of such knightly tolerance in recent times was perhaps G. K. Chesterton.

The same ethical foundation on which the principle of tolerance rests also defines and justifies its necessary limitations. Virtuous tolerance is least of all a limitless *laissez faire*. The love that invites us to serve the objective good of our fellow-man asks us at the same time not only to respect the other's freedom but also to protect that freedom against all unjust and violent attacks. No matter how one of our fellow-men may subjectively try to justify an attitude of intolerance, by which he believes he has the right to oppress the free utterances of opinion and conviction of his fellow-men, tolerance by its own inner logic sees itself obliged to offer opposition to it. He who accepts respect for the human person as a guide of conduct, must accept all the imperatives that follow from it according to the circumstances. The same motive that inspires his tolerance obliges him to offer relentless resistance and opposition to intolerance. Precisely in virtue of the principle of tolerance there is, therefore, something which the tolerant man can never tolerate, namely, that others would follow a plan of life which does harm to the freedom of their fellow-men. With such persons the tolerant man must not only speak and argue, but he is also obliged to counteract their violence as much as possible and prevent the propaganda of ideologies that preach such violence.

Hence tolerance does not exclude every ideological battle that is fought with the weapons of force. Freedom in our earthly community of persons is a universal condition of the common good. As such, it must take away from the members of that community all freedom to combat freedom. Liberty, as belonging to the common good, excludes every action of particular freedom that is directed against freedom. Those who are responsible for the common good—this includes fundamentally all citizens and formally the bearers of authority in the community—must repress the expressions of particular freedom that are directed against the right of liberty of members, whatever might be the ideological reasons offered for those expressions.

After this fundamental clarification of tolerance it is not difficult to determine its implications as a socio-ethical principle. According to this principle, every society must practice tolerance in the above-explained sense with respect to its members and the subordinate groups existing in it, as well as toward coordinated groups existing side by side with it. The difficulties begin only when the principle is applied to various kinds of human societies. For the application of this socio-ethical principle is not only limited interiorly by the duty of opposition to active intolerance, but also by the fact that certain societies are based on the common acceptance of particular convictions. Hence it is necessary to make, first, a distinction between what we may call, in a broad sense, "natural" societies and others that originate through a special institution. Societies are "natural" if they are based on the very nature of man, either primarily as in the case of the family, or secondarily as in that of the state.

Wherever man appears in nature, he is in some way connected with a family. This connection can be unicellular as in the ordinary family, multicellular as in the "joint family" whose members may live together or scattered, and it can even extend to a clan or a tribe. The closer man is to pure nature, the more the family is the principal or even the exclusive form of community.

The state is only a secondary natural community. It is characterized by authority or the exercise of institutional power, and it appears only later in mankind's historical development. Modern sociologists believe that it is not more than ten thousand years old. Hence the state is a rather recent phenomenon. It is the product of human culture and striving for power. Sometimes it came about through an opportune seizure of power which fixed a historical situation arising from an inner cultural development; sometimes it was the result of an agreement inspired by a common understanding, a common need, a common place of pilgrimage, etc. Often also it resulted, unfortunately, from the violent subjection of one or more peoples to a conquering nation. Nevertheless, the creation of the state seems to be inevitable in the development of the human community.

That development eventually reaches a stage where the unity, within which men depend on one another economically and culturally, is so all-embracing and the problems are so manifold and difficult, that an orderly prolongation and development of the life of the community is possible only under the guidance of an institutional organization of power. In this sense the state is a secondary natural form of society. It is also secondary in the sense that it can ethically justify its existence only insofar as it is necessarily required for the good of the homogenous or mixed community of peoples that constitute the domain of its authority. The state exists for the sake of the community that has organically developed from the family, which is the primary natural community.

It is proper to natural societies that they are not *per se* based on some common view of the world. However, though rooted in nature, they are associations of men whose existence is a task directed to the fulfillment of an ideal meaning of life. For this reason it is normal that their social activity should be guided by a common view of life. The fact that, e.g., grownup children come to a different view of life than that of the family in which they were born and raised, or that in a religiously homogeneous nation there develop minorities of people who think differently, is a source of unrest and dangerous tensions for those communities. These tensions can become salutary only if those societies' members listen to and act upon the invitation to tolerance involved in the new situation, and thus reach a higher degree of humanity. Men generally do not rise to higher achievements except by victories of the spirit over the difficulties that present themselves in historical situations. Spiritual division, however, is never a good in itself, although in mankind's long historical progress it may be practically a necessity for the purification of the soul. But the ideal remains unity of the human community of persons in truth.

Regarding tolerance in natural societies, we can say in general that it is simply obligatory; hence its only limitations are those imposed upon tolerance by its own nature. There is, of course, growth in ethical consciousness during mankind's historical development. It is only in our own time that the full ethical range and import of tolerance has begun to enter into the conscience of the world. This we must take into account when we judge the past and some of the situations that still exist in our present world.

In a general discussion such as this, it is not necessary to explain in detail what are the concrete demands of tolerance in the various forms of the natural human society. However, it is useful to say a few words about the state. The tolerance of public power in respect to the citizens and associations existing in the state, is called "civil tolerance." It is exercised in the laws, regulations and activities of the civil power as such. That the civil power must obey the demands of tolerance in the exercise of its authority follows from the fact that the state is by its very nature subsidiary with respect to the living natural community whose juridical order it maintains and defends by the exercise of power. Now tolerance is a fundamental ethical principle of that natural society, hence the state is obliged to obey its demands. The state has no commission to teach or force any view of the world and life upon its citizens. Its task is to protect the freedom of the citizens and social groups according to justice and, within the limits of law, to foster the development of those objective cultural means that will enable the citizens to strive in a spirit of solidarity for the fulfillment of their human task of life according to the ideals of their consciences.

171

It is the duty of the state to be impartial with respect to the spiritual divergencies of its citizens and to distribute the burdens and benefits among the various groups according to the demands of distributive and social justice.

From the ordinary family the natural community complex spreads out into ever widening circles of associations to embrace the whole of mankind. The circle within which the solidarity of men expresses its demands effectively keeps growing in virtue of the total development of culture. It ultimately tends to encompass the whole of mankind. Although the historico-dialectical progress of culture is activated by men's freedom and will, it is not the will that causes the broadening of the domain of solidarity. This widening is the result of the total historical development in which man's will is only one factor. In other words, the constantly widening circle of effective solidarity is not produced by a deliberate act of will but grows. The domain within which men's natural solidarity tends to become ever wider is a product of the progress of culture. The fact that man belongs to this particular family and to that particular historical community, whether great or small, is determined by his birth.

However, within that growing natural society, the free choice of men brings all sorts of economic, cultural and religious associations into being by institution. The state itself came into being by an act of institution but, given certain circumstances, it is a necessary form that organizes the complex whole of natural society. That is why we called the state a secondary natural society. Accordingly, within the natural complex that is organized as a state in one of its many forms, there arise all sorts of societies through institution for the pursuit of specific purposes.

Among these institutions there are some whose common good is a value to which one can direct oneself only in virtue of a particular world view or of particular ideas concerning society. Among these special mention must be made of religious associations, such as Christian churches and religious orders, or other *weltanschauliche* societies, such as the American Humanist Association. Man does not belong to those societies by nature, in virtue of his birth, but by an act of free choice. He continues to be a member because he continues to be inspired by the same conviction that justified his joining those societies. He can leave such a group whenever he wishes without thereby ceasing to be a member of the natural community to which he belongs by nature. Many questions arise with respect to these statements, which cannot all be dealt with here. One example of such a problem arises for many Christian communities from the position that one becomes a member of their church through baptism. But baptism is a sacrament of faith, and the man who is mentally mature does not remain a member of the church in virtue of his baptism if he renounces it by a conscious rejection of the faith. Even the mature Catholic remains a member of his church only in virtue of a free assent of faith.

In purely conventional societies, to which man can belong only through his free choice and because of some conviction to which he is bound and in which he binds himself to others, there can be no question, of course, of tolerance regarding the view of life that belongs to the binding faith of the group. To remain in such a group and participate in its internal activities one must adhere to and profess the common faith of the group. If one of the members publicly attacks a conviction that belongs to the binding foundation of the group, the latter has the right and often even the obligation to condemn and, if the member persists, to express publicly the expulsion of that member through the voice of its leaders. We do not mean, of course, that the leaders have the right to use physical or moral force against the member to make him recant his new conviction. For instance, the society is not permitted to order that he be deprived of the means necessary for his personal life because the natural community, by virtue of natural solidarity, owes those means to all persons that are living in its fold. A society based on a conviction may only deny him its own specific means, the means that are directed to the special purpose which derives its meaning from the conviction on which it is based. This is done, for instance, by the Catholic Church, when it denies someone its sacraments and means of salvation.

It is also evident that a religious order based on the vows of religion cannot retain and suffer to remain in itself a member who publicly attacks the value to which those vows tend. It would lead us too far afield to enter into details about the many possibilities that can occur in this matter. Let us merely insist that a most generous tolerance must reign also in those instituted communities with respect to all the points which, within a particular community, belong to the domain of free opinion. For example, it would be contrary to the ethical imperative of tolerance if a church authority proclaimed condemnations and excommunications for theological or other opinions which are not very clearly in opposition to the truth which is entrusted to the church as a fundamental belief of the community. This should be evident to a Christian. For the new law, as St. Thomas expressed it, is "the law of perfect freedom" because it does not impose anything on its members that is not really obligatory for salvation.[6]

5. Conclusion

The three socio-ethical principles we have discussed must not only be distinguished but also understood in their unity and their interconnection. They are not only radically one, as different socio-ethical expressions of the one ethical absolute of love, but are also connected with one another in their practical exercise and in their orientation to one and the same goal, the realization of the common good. As we have already shown, the principle of subsidiarity presupposes and intrinsically completes the dynamic imperative of solidarity. The principle of tolerance means that the existence of diverse views of life, socially expressed in particular associations and undertakings, does not exclude the effective solidarity of the general community. The demands that spring from

[6]*Summa Theologica,* p. I-II, a. 108, q. 1, c and *ad* 2.

solidarity and subsidiarity are not enervated nor diminished because there exist particular groups that are separated from one another by differences in their views of life. This too belongs to the ethical imperative of tolerance when we consider it in the total context of the social ethos.

The solidarity and subsidiarity of persons and groups within the human community, taken absolutely, transcend and bridge the opposition flowing from the views of life held by particular groups. Solidarity and subsidiarity, then, must find expression in a harmonious collaboration for the general good of the human community. This collaboration can find expression in a variety of mixed groups and associations.

In principle, persons belonging to diverse confessions can work together in all associations whose aim is not conditioned by their own faith. The same applies to the cooperation of various ideological groups by means of mixed societies and organizations. Catholics, Protestants, Jews and humanists can, in principle, cooperate with perfect freedom and solidarity in institutions or associations directed to economic, social, and political purposes or to the exercise of science, art and other cultural activities. This assertion applies also to institutions of learning and education if the student who entrusts himself to them or is entrusted to them by his parents receives the guarantee that, within the total pedagogical pattern, the initiation into the tradition of culture will be sufficiently adjusted to the demands of his own faith.

Considered in itself, the ideal for a pluralist community lies in an open community life in which the groups do not live as juxtaposed closed units. That which unites them should be expressed socially and organizationally and pursued together just as much as that in which they differ from one another. This is a demand made by the universal solidarity and brotherhood of man. However, the concrete situation, which is also determined by all sorts of ethically reprehensible factors, does not always permit the realization of that which is *per se* desirable. The measure in which the ideal can actually be realized will depend precisely on the measure in which ethical tolerance will have molded the spirit of the diverse groups and purified the situations. What should be done here and now must always be determined in the light of the whole constellation of human circumstances. But it should be done with a preference for openness. He who unites solidarity and tolerance in one attitude will always strive for a maximum of unity in the social fabric. He will try to prepare the way for the most perfect social expression of what unites men as men on earth.

INDEX OF NAMES

INDEX OF SUBJECT MATTER

178